ASTON MARTIN
DB9 and VANQUISH

THE COMPLETE STORY

TITLES IN THE CROWOOD AUTOCLASSICS SERIES

Alfa Romeo 105 Series Spider
Alfa Romeo 916 GTV & Spider
Alfa Romeo 2000 and 2600
Alfa Romeo Alfasud
Aston Martin DB7
Aston Martin DB9 and Vanquish
Aston Martin V8
BMW E30
BMW M3
BMW M5
BMW Z3 and Z4
Classic Jaguar XK – The Six-Cylinder Cars
Classic Mini Specials and Moke
Ferrari 308, 328 & 348
Frogeye Sprite
Ginetta: Road & Track Cars
Jaguar E-Type
Jaguar F-Type
Jaguar Mks 1 & 2, S-Type & 420
Jaguar XJ-S
Jensen V8
Lamborghini Diablo
Land Rover Discovery
Land Rover Freelander
Lotus Elan
Lotus Elise & Exige 1995–2020
Lotus Esprit
MGA
MGB
Mazda MX-5
Mercedes-Benz 'Fintail' Models
Mercedes-Benz Pontons
Mercedes-Benz S-Class 1972–2013
Mercedes SL Series
Mercedes-Benz SL & SLC 107 Series
Mercedes-Benz Saloon Coupé
Mercedes-Benz W123
Mercedes-Benz W124
Mercedes-Benz W126 S-Class 1979–1991
Mercedes-Benz W201 (190)
Mercedes W113
Morgan 4/4: The First 75 Years
Morgan Plus 8
NSU Ro 80
Peugeot 205
Porsche 924/928/944/968
Porsche Boxster and Cayman
Porsche Carrera – The Air-Cooled Era 1953–1998
Porsche Air-Cooled Turbos 1974–1996
Porsche Carrera - The Water-Cooled Era 1998–2018
Porsche Water-Cooled Turbos 1979–2019
Range Rover First Generation
Range Rover Second Generation
Range Rover Sport 2005–2013
Range Rover Third Generation
Reliant Three-Wheelers
Rolls-Royce Silver Cloud
Rover 800 Series
Rover P5 & P5B
Rover P6: 2000, 2200, 3500
Rover SDI
Saab 92-96V4
Saab 99 and 900
Shelby and AC Cobra
Toyota MR2
Triumph Spitfire and GT6
Triumph TR6
TVR 1946–1982
TVR Cars of the Peter Wheeler Era
Volkswagen Karmann Ghia and Cabriolet
Volvo 1800
Volvo Amazon

ASTON MARTIN DB9 and VANQUISH

THE COMPLETE STORY

JAMES TAYLOR

THE CROWOOD PRESS

First published in 2024 by
The Crowood Press Ltd
Ramsbury, Marlborough
Wiltshire SN8 2HR

enquiries@crowood.com

www.crowood.com

British Library Cataloguing-in-Publication Data
A catalogue record for this book is available from the British Library.

ISBN 978 0 7198 4316 7

Typeset by Chennai Publishing Services

Cover design by Blue Sunflower Creative

Printed and bound in India by Parksons Graphics Pvt Ltd

CONTENTS

INTRODUCTION AND ACKNOWLEDGEMENTS

The Aston Martin name conjures up images of glamorous high-performance machinery, and rightly so. Despite a difficult period – one of many in the company's lifetime – in the later years of the twentieth century, the marque reinvented itself with stunning success at the start of the new century. The New Era cars were spearheaded by the Vanquish, which set the tone for the models to follow with its timeless shape and superb V12 engine. Within a couple of years of its 2001 launch, it had been promoted to the position of range flagship and had been joined by a less expensive but no less exciting model called the DB9.

These are the cars covered by this book, which also takes a brief look at the short-lived Virage that was intended to fill a position between them in the market. Although newer models have now taken their place in Aston Martin showrooms, there remains considerable respect for the Vanquish and DB9, which have slid seamlessly into the category of modern classics.

Telling their story has been a fascinating experience, but it could not have been done successfully without the kind assistance of the Aston Martin Heritage Trust. For many of the pictures used in this book I have drawn on Aston Martin's own publicity material, and to supplement that I have added a few of my own photographs and a number drawn from social media, whose originators have kindly made them available for further use. I am very grateful to them all.

James Taylor
Oxfordshire
April 2023

TIMELINE

	Vanquish	DB9
1998	Project Vantage concept at Detroit Show	
2001	Launch at Geneva (March)	
2002	Appears in *Die Another Day*, a 007 film	
2003	Sports Dynamic Pack available	Launch at Frankfurt Show
2004	Vanquish Zagato Roadster Vanquish S	Volante introduced
2005		Racing DBR9 and DBRS9 introduced
2006	Last Vanquish built	Sports pack available
2007	Boniolo Vanquish EG Shooting Brake	GT1 Class win at Le Mans
2008		Le Mans edition Facelift for 2009 season
2010		Minor facelift for 2011 season
2011		Carbon Black, Morning Frost and Quantum Silver editions
2012		Major improvements for 2013 season
2013		DB9 Hybrid (May) Spyder Zagato Centennial (July)
2014		Carbon edition (March)
2015		DB9 GT introduced (June) GT Bond edition (September)
2016		'Last of 9' edition and end of production (July)

CHAPTER 1

ASTON MARTIN, THE COMPANY

When the wealthy and successful British tractor manufacturer David Brown bought Aston Martin for £20,500 in 1947, he was both indulging a whim and getting a bargain. The Aston Martin company had reached a low point in its existence – so low, in fact, that it had offered itself for sale through a classified advertisement in *The Times* newspaper as a 'high-class motor business'.

David Brown, clearly in acquisitive mood, bought the ailing Lagonda company later the same year for a further £52,500. He merged the two companies into one, renaming it Aston Martin Lagonda Ltd, and setting it up in new premises at Hanworth Park in Feltham, Middlesex, not far from its earlier factory. Here, he had his engineers draw up the first of the new company's cars. They would bear his initials to distinguish them from those that had gone before, and would become the first of the legendary DB-series Aston Martins.

In Aston Martin, what David Brown was buying was indeed a 'high-class motor business', even though it was a small one. The company had developed a formidable reputation as a maker of high-performance sporting machinery, but it had never really made much money, and the disruption of the 1939–1945 war, when the Aston Martin works had been commandeered by the Air Ministry for the manufacture of aircraft parts, had certainly not helped.

The highly recognisable winged Aston Martin emblem is seen here on the nose of a DB2/4 dating from the 1950s.

The original Aston Martin company had been founded in 1913 by Lionel Martin, a wealthy car enthusiast, and Robert Bamford, an engineer. Since 1912, the two had been in business as Bamford & Martin, with premises in London's Callow Street from which they sold Singer cars and serviced other makes, including GWK and Calthorpe. Lionel Martin had a Singer-based 'special' that he raced enthusiastically at Aston Hill, near Aston Clinton in Buckinghamshire, and when the partners decided to try making their own car, the combination of the Aston and Martin names was a natural choice.

The first Aston Martin was another 'special', this time with a Coventry-Simplex engine in a 1908 Isotta-Fraschini voiturette racing chassis. By March 1915, Bamford and Martin had their own design ready, and they also had new premises at Henniker Mews in Kensington – but the Great War had broken out a year earlier. Both men were called to serve their country, and all the original Aston Martin equipment and machinery was sold to the Sopwith Aviation Company.

Undeterred, the two got together again after the war, and by 1920 they were in business at Abingdon Road in Kensington. From 1921 the company had its Aston Martin Special Sports in low-volume production, but Robert Bamford had already left. Despite an injection of funds from the wealthy amateur racing driver Count Louis Zborowski, and in spite of some notable successes in major race events, Aston Martin went bankrupt in 1924. It was bought by Lady Charnwood, and staggered on for another year before failing again. In 1926 the factory closed and Lionel Martin left the business – but later that year Lady Charnwood and a group of investors revitalised the company and relocated it to Feltham, where it moved into the Victoria Road premises formerly occupied by the Whitehead Aircraft Company.

Key among the investors in the new company were Bill Renwick and Augustus ('Bert') Bertelli, who had previously been partners in an automotive business and now brought their ideas to bear on the future of Aston Martin. Though production levels were always low – an Aston Martin was a more or less bespoke creation intended for those who had the means to indulge in the fashionable sport of motor racing – the company gained a formidable reputation through racing successes. It was this reputation that persuaded one investor after another to keep the company alive when it failed yet again in 1932. But by 1936 it had become clear that the company could not remain profitable if it focused so heavily on competition machinery. That year a decision was made to focus on road cars, and as a consequence production was increased to over 200 cars a year for the rest of the 1930s.

In 1939, Aston Martin looked at expanding production by adding a smaller car to its portfolio, a little sports saloon with lightweight aluminium bodywork called the Atom. However, that project was necessarily suspended during the war years, and although it was revived with a new engine when peace came, Aston Martin floundered for a while. Even though buyers were grateful to get their hands on any kind of car at all during the years of austerity that immediately followed the war, the economic circumstances of the time did not favour expensive and individualistic performance types.

THE DAVID BROWN CARS

The first car to come from the Feltham works under its new post-war ownership was called the DB1, and it was a little tentative (which was understandable in view of the times) and more than a little odd in appearance. However, it was the next car that demonstrated the wisdom of David Brown's purchases. In 1949 he entered a new car at Le Mans that combined the 6-cylinder Lagonda engine (designed by W.O. Bentley) with an aerodynamic coupé body based on a space-frame of square-section tubes. The following year this entered production as the DB2, and it pointed the way ahead for Aston Martin.

Available as a 107bhp DB2 or a 123bhp DB2 Vantage (the first use of a name that would become famous), the new car was a grand touring coupé that was wholly capable of being used as a track racer if its owner so wished. It was noisy, cramped inside, and not quite as able on the track as subsequent legend would have it, but it undoubtedly looked the part and (quite literally) made all the right noises. It was also considerably more robust and better built than most of the hand-crafted Italian cars that were its natural competitors.

The Aston Martin Atom never made production, although prototypes were produced from 1939 to 1944. It was a little sports saloon designed to bring the company wider sales.

The DB1 was the first post-war production Aston Martin. Though not particularly attractive, it made its own statement about the company's performance intentions.

The DB2 coupé defined Aston Martin very well in the early 1950s. The shape was exquisite, despite that huge air intake just below the number-plate.

Tidied up visually, and with more power and more seats (although rear accommodation was still an afterthought), the DB2/4 of 1952 continued with the same successful overall appearance.

Sporting intent: though very much an early 1950s design, the DB2/4 looked powerful from every angle.

Those who wanted open-air motoring were certainly not ignored, and this elegant and desirable machine is the drophead coupé variant of the DB2/4.

Racing certainly improves the breed ... and this is the 1956 DBR1, a sports racing model designed to compete in the World Sportscar Championship. In 1959 it won both that Championship and the 24 Hours of Le Mans; pictured is the actual Le Mans winner.

Aston Martin followed up with a 'works' racing programme that helped gain publicity for the cars. Some dedicated racing cars appeared: the DB3 in 1952, followed by the DB3S a year later. Meanwhile the DB2 evolved into an occasional four-seater (the 1952 DB2/4), its original 2.6-litre engine was increased in size to 3 litres, and a rather stylish drophead body was offered alongside the original coupé. The DB2/4 MkII followed in 1955 with more power and a new fixed-head coupé body, and then in 1957 the further developed DB MkIII arrived. It was this model that, amongst other things, introduced a new front grille shape that would go on to become an Aston Martin visual trademark.

THE MOVE TO NEWPORT PAGNELL

The Astons of the early 1950s were not assembled at the company's premises in Feltham, but at the premises of the coachbuilder Tickford at Newport Pagnell in Buckinghamshire. The chassis were constructed at the David Brown works in Farsley, Yorkshire, while the bodies were being built by Mulliners of Birmingham. The two came together at the Tickford works, where the bodies were painted and trimmed before being mated to the chassis to create complete cars. For the Tickford company, the Aston Martin contract was important business, and very necessary as the market for bespoke coachbuilt bodies gradually shrank.

When Tickford's ran into financial trouble in 1954 it was almost automatic for David Brown to buy the company. From early 1955 the Newport Pagnell factory was turned over entirely to work for Aston Martin and Lagonda, and it became the company's assembly plant. The Aston Martin engineering and test departments, and the administrative offices, would remain at Feltham for a few more years, but gradually all these functions were centred on Newport Pagnell. So the DB4, new in 1958, became the first Aston Martin to be manufactured and assembled wholly at Newport Pagnell. Even so, the cars continued to wear identification plates that gave the Feltham address for many more years. Aston Martin Lagonda finally left its old Middlesex home in 1964, by which time DB4 production had ended and had given way to that of the DB5. Aston Martin Works, the company's heritage division, remains at Newport Pagnell to this day.

Meanwhile, Italian styling had come to the fore in Europe, and was even attracting interest from American car makers as well. Italian cars were also making a major impact as motor sport returned to the agenda in the early 1950s, and David Brown was shrewd enough not only to consider the

Now with Italian styling to add to their charms, the Astons of the 1960s were spearheaded by the DB4. This is the short-wheelbase DB4 GT, a superbly balanced design.

Italians purely as the sporting opposition, but to embrace what they had to offer. Aston Martin sent three of the DB2/4 MkII chassis to Carrozzeria Touring in Milan to be given 'spider' (open sports) bodies. It was the start of an association that would stand Aston Martin in good stead; later, Touring would play a part in developing the Superleggera bodywork of the DB4 model.

THE CLASSIC ERA

Over the next decade and a half, Aston Martin created some remarkably capable, devastatingly attractive, and much lauded sports cars. They had their faults: they were typically rather heavy despite the extensive use of aluminium alloys in their bodies, and they tended to be rather brutal in contrast with the delicacy of many Italian-made rivals. Yet the 1958 DB4, 1963 DB5 and 1965 DB6 created a legend that endures to this day. The cars all depended on coachwork designed by Touring in Milan, and all were powered by derivatives of a twin-overhead-camshaft 6-cylinder engine designed by engineer Tadek Marek in the mid-1950s.

It was during this period that Aston Martin also made one of its smartest business moves ever. The first James Bond 007 film based on Ian Fleming's novels about the fictional British professional spy was a massive box-office hit during 1962, and the team behind it followed up with a second film in 1963. A third was soon in the planning, and for this the production company wanted a glamorous car for the hero to drive. Jaguar turned them down, but Aston Martin were just about to release the DB5 and agreed to provide a pair of cars for filming.

The original script only called for the car to be fitted with a device to create a smokescreen that would hinder pursuing vehicles, but the fertile minds on the production team added an array of gadgets that included a revolving licence plate, an ejector seat, and machine guns concealed behind the sidelights. When the film *Goldfinger* appeared in 1964, the resulting publicity for the DB5 was enormous. A special scale model made by Corgi Toys became a huge hit as well, and from then on the name of Aston Martin became inseparable from the James Bond 007 franchise. Even though other car makers have had their moments in the sun too, the DB5 appeared in six more James Bond films – first *Thunderball* in 1965, and then, after a pause, *Goldeneye* (1995), *Tomorrow Never Dies* (1997), *Casino Royale* (2006), *Skyfall* (2012) and *Spectre* (2015). Aston Martin has exploited the connection ever since.

Aston's first great classic era was brought to a close with the DBS, which was originally intended to have a V8 engine but instead took on the 4-litre 6-cylinder from the DB6 when the new engine was not ready in time. Even though a more powerful DBS Vantage was offered, the car suffered criticism for not delivering performance significantly better

The car that took Aston Martin into the public consciousness was the DB5, best known as the car from the James Bond 007 film *Goldfinger*. This is a standard 1965 DB5 coupé, without the special gadgets added to the film car.

The 6-cylinder twin-overhead-camshaft engine of the DB5 was impressive to look at as well as being a superb performer.

The DB6 continued the lines already established by the DB4 and DB5. This Volante convertible derivative is seen with its folding top erected.

than its predecessor. Despite its stylish new body designed by William Towns, which maintained the classic coupé proportions but was slick in the latest idiom, and despite a new De Dion rear suspension to improve the handling, the DBS was not entirely what Aston Martin customers wanted. It nevertheless took the company to the end of what is still sometimes seen as its best decade.

THE UNHAPPY YEARS

The DBS got its much awaited V8 engine in 1970: a 5.3-litre all-alloy unit designed by Tadek Marek that put out around 350bhp on its introduction. The car was renamed a DBS V8 and proved brutally fast, but that was not quite enough to win back the customers who had gone elsewhere at the end of the 1960s. The Bosch fuel-injection system on early models needed careful maintenance, and fuel consumption could be alarmingly high if the cars were used as their makers expected. However, before much could be done about these early disappointments, a great deal went wrong for Aston Martin.

The problems began in 1972 when financial trouble obliged David Brown to sell both his tractor company and Aston Martin Lagonda. Although Ford showed some interest, the car company was sold to Company Developments Ltd, who did as their reputation suggested they would and began to slim down the company in order to maximise profits. A year later, the first oil crisis sent the prices of petrol at the pumps sky high, and large and thirsty cars of all types became hard to sell. Aston Martin was soon in trouble, as sales tumbled and the quality of its products fell thanks to cost cutting by its new owners.

Company Developments responded by creating a two-model range that was intended to bring in the buyers. The DBS V8 evolved into the AM V8 and its price was increased by over 25 per cent, while a cheaper model called the Vantage was introduced, using the old 6-cylinder engine of the DBS in the latest body. The customers were not impressed with either model, and only 70 of the Vantage were made before Aston Martin entered receivership at the end of 1974.

A consortium of businessmen bought the company from the receiver in 1975 and began trading again as Aston Martin Lagonda (1975) Ltd. They retained the DBS V8 model, which staggered on through several improvements as the Aston Martin V8 saloon until 1989, all the while becoming increasingly dated. Against that background, the company hatched a bold plan to produce a car that would appeal strongly to the emerging taste for Western luxury goods in Middle Eastern markets.

That car was announced in 1976 as the Aston Martin Lagonda, although actual production did not begin until 1978. Powered by the V8 engine, and stuffed full of what seemed like avant-garde technology at the time, this four-door saloon had unforgettable wedge-shaped styling by William Towns. To some eyes it was simply garish, but it was a major hit with the media and put the Aston Martin name in the spotlight once again. The company attempted a second bite of the cherry with the Bulldog coupé concept in 1979, with another wedge shape from Towns and a 600bhp twin-turbocharged derivative of their V8 engine. Not quite capable of reaching its 320km/h (200mph) target, the car nevertheless achieved 307km/h (191mph) on test and gained more valuable publicity for Aston Martin, although cost considerations ensured that it would never go into production.

Meanwhile the company soldiered on through the end of the 1970s and into the 1980s with its V8-powered coupés in a quite bewildering variety of forms, which included a Vantage model that in 1977 returned the use of the name to its traditional position for a high-performance derivative. From mid-1978 there was a Volante convertible derivative too, and with the performance enhancements this had the full title of Aston Martin V8 Vantage Volante.

THE VICTOR GAUNTLETT YEARS

By the end of the 1970s, Aston Martin's outlook was bleak. Worldwide sales had dropped to 150 cars a year, and production was no longer sustainable. However, in 1980 the company was rescued by investments from Victor Gauntlett of Pace Petroleum, a long-time car enthusiast, and Tim Hearley of CH Industrials. They took over as joint owners in early 1981, when Gauntlett became Executive Chairman.

An energetic few years followed, with sponsorship of racing at AMOC events and the development of a Group C racer (the Nimrod), which came third in the Manufacturers' Championship in both 1982 and 1983 and also finished seventh in the 1982 24 Hours of Le Mans. The lack of new production models was beginning to tell, however, and Aston Martin built just 30 cars to meet demand in 1982. Trading conditions persuaded Gauntlett to sell Pace Petroleum in September 1983, while he sold his share in Aston Martin to the Greek shipping tycoon Peter Livanos. Gauntlett nevertheless remained as Aston Martin Chairman.

The 1988 Virage was Aston's first new car in twenty years, and it set the style for the big and brutal coupés of the following decade.

Victor Gauntlett, Aston Martin Chairman from 1981 to 1991, kept the company alive and relevant during a difficult period. He is standing in front of one of the Zagato cars he commissioned.

The 1980s were characterised by speculation and see-sawing prices in all fields, and by a new appetite for making money quickly. Changing social expectations also saw a major change in the demographic of Aston Martin buyers. Once characterised as the tweedy country set (at least in Britain), they were now increasingly bankers, entrepreneurs, lawyers and others who had found a way to attract wealth in the new situation. An Aston Martin became a symbol of that wealth as much as an expression of individuality. Meanwhile the models no longer in production attained the status of investments.

The company rose to the occasion. Chasing sales but remaining as true as possible to its own traditions, it commissioned the Italian coachbuilder Zagato (in which Victor Gauntlett had bought an interest) to design a sleek if somewhat angular coupé body for a shortened version of the existing V8-engined chassis. With a 430bhp version of the engine, it was claimed the car was capable of 300km/h (186mph). It was announced at the 1986 Geneva Show, but only as a drawing, and yet it immediately attracted orders. The original coupé sold just 52 copies before being withdrawn in 1990, and its production coincided with a peak in speculation on supercars from which Aston Martin drew benefit. A convertible version followed, of which just 37 examples were built.

The success of the Zagato car helped provide the funds for Aston Martin to develop its first new car in twenty years, which was announced in 1988 as the Virage. Its V8 engine had been reworked by Callaway Engineering in the USA, with a 4-valve design that maintained outputs and performance in the face of increasingly tightening emissions requirements. The body was a sleek and curvaceous design with the classic coupé profile that had been drawn up by John Heffernan and Ken Greenley, who were automotive design tutors at the Royal College of Art in London. Meanwhile the chassis was the final version of the one designed by Harold Beach for the DB4, more than 30 years earlier.

FORD OWNERSHIP

In the meantime, another new chapter in the history of Aston Martin was about to begin. By the mid-1980s Gauntlett had recognised that the company needed a major injection of capital to safeguard its long-term future, and mentioned this at a chance meeting with Walter Hayes, Vice President of Ford of Europe. Hayes saw the potential of the brand, and after negotiations with the then owners, Ford bought a 75 per cent stake in Aston Martin in September 1987.

Once they had reviewed the situation, Ford concluded that Aston Martin needed a new model that was less expensive than the Virage, as quickly as possible. This was going to require the sort of major engineering input that only Ford could provide, and as a result the American company acquired the remaining 25 per cent stake in Aston Martin during 1988. In 1991, Walter Hayes took over from Victor Gauntlett as the company's Chairman.

Meanwhile events at Ford-owned Jaguar helped to shape the plans for a new Aston Martin. During 1990, Ford cancelled Jaguar's planned F-type sports car. Tom Walkinshaw of TWR suggested building a new Jaguar on the existing XJ-S platform, and asked his own designer Ian Callum to draw up a suitable body shape. Jaguar rejected this, but Walter Hayes realised that it represented a cost-effective way of providing Aston Martin with the new model it needed. He asked Callum to modify his design to make it suitable for an Aston Martin, and had TWR at Kidlington undertake the necessary engineering, supercharging and re-working of a 6-cylinder Jaguar engine for the job.

The new model returned to earlier nomenclature, and took on the name of DB7. It was presented at the Geneva Show in 1993, and the following year production began at the factory in Banbury Road, Bloxham, where the Jaguar XJ220 had earlier been built. Anticipated production quantities were far greater than the old Newport Pagnell works could accommodate, although this remained active for production of the Virage. The DB7 became the only Aston Martin to have a steel monocoque construction, which was inherited from Jaguar: later models would depend on the lightweight aluminium that had been traditional to the earlier DB series cars.

Sales of the DB7 confirmed the wisdom of Ford's decision to put the model into production. In 1995, Aston Martin produced 700 cars (including Virage models), which was more than at any time in its history. In 1997, a DB7 Volante convertible joined the coupé model in production, and in 1998 the company built the 2,000th example of the DB7. All this was achieved while maintaining the high degree of hand-building that had been an essential part of the Aston Martin image.

There was no Vantage specification yet, but that was in preparation, and in 1999 the DB7 Vantage was released with the superb new V12 engine that had been developed from a design by Ford in the USA. (There is more about the origins of this engine in Chapter 2.) This car proved such an

The DB range was continued under Ford ownership with the DB7, which may have had a lot of Jaguar in it but was nevertheless a very worthy Aston Martin. This is a DB7 GT, with the 6-cylinder engine.

The new V12 engine made its first appearance in the DB7 Vantage, and made very clear that Aston Martin now had a worthy powerplant of their own to take them through the first years of the new century.

immediate hit that the 6-cylinder version of the DB7 became virtually unsaleable and was discontinued later in the year. The DB7 as a model remained in production until 2004, by which time 7,000 examples had been built. At that time, it was the most numerous Aston Martin ever made – but subsequent models would eclipse it.

A NEW ERA, AND NEW OWNERS AGAIN

By this time, the era of Aston Martin's history that is covered in this book had begun. As the chapters that follow make clear, Ford invested massively in both a new engine and in new structural technology to create a new platform, and together these achieved their purpose of propelling the Aston Martin brand back to the top of the supercar desirability charts. The first of the new high-tech models was the Vanquish, which was introduced in 2001 as a replacement for the top model Virage, and, after earlier product proposals had been rejected, the replacement for the DB7 was announced in 2003 as the DB9 (and not the DB8, for reasons explained in Chapter 5).

The new platform, which originated with the Vanquish but had been further developed into a modular type by the time of the DB9, would go on to serve Aston Martin for nearly thirteen years and would underpin every new model between 2003 and 2016. And yet this advanced engineering technology was not enough to keep Aston Martin entirely out of difficulties, through no fault of the company's new CEO, Dr Ulrich Bez, who had been put in place by Ford in mid-2000. While the models described in this book were in production, a somewhat turbulent business story was playing out in the background.

The new headquarters at Gaydon replaced both the former Jaguar-TWR plant that had been home to the DB7 and the older Newport Pagnell assembly plant.

A key figure in Aston Martin's revival at the start of the 21st century was Dr Ulrich Bez.

THE ULRICH BEZ LEGACY

Dr Ulrich Bez was a major influence on the Aston Martin marque in the period when the Vanquish and DB9 were in production. He joined Aston Martin in July 2000 as its Chief Executive Officer, and stood down from that role in April 2013. He then remained with Aston Martin as non-executive Chairman, taking over from David Richards.

Bez had been appointed to turn Aston Martin around, and in his thirteen years as CEO he had achieved exactly that. Under his leadership, Aston Martin had developed into a globally acclaimed luxury brand. It had launched no fewer than twenty major models, as well as some remarkable concepts, and it had made a successful return to motor sport. In the Bez years, Aston Martin had sold over 50,000 cars, which was more than three times as many as it had sold in the 87 years between its foundation in 1913 and his arrival in 2000.

In 2013 Bez published a book, *Making Aston Martin*, which describes his background as well as his work at Aston Martin.

It sometimes seemed that things were never destined to go smoothly for Aston Martin. Just as the company seemed to have a coherent model range in place and an assured future, owner Ford began to seek significant economies across its global interests. This was the result of a major internal audit, which revealed that action needed to be taken immediately; among the early casualties was the Premier Automotive Group of European brands to which Aston Martin belonged. Beginning in 2006, the various marques were sold off: Volvo went to Geely in China, Jaguar and Land Rover were sold to Tata in India, and in August 2006 Ford announced it had engaged UBS AG to sell all or part of Aston Martin at auction.

On 12 March 2007 a consortium led by David Richards, the Chairman of British motor-sport company Prodrive, bought a majority holding in Aston Martin from Ford for £475 million. Ford retained a £40 million stake in the company. The consortium included a US investment banker and two Kuwaiti companies, but there was no direct involvement from Prodrive itself. Plans for future expansion were already in place, and Dr Ulrich Bez, who remained as Chief Executive Officer, stated in an interview that year that he believed Aston Martin needed to become more visible and build more cars. The company hoped to sell 7,000 cars during 2007, and in particular wanted to expand its sales in Italy, where it would take on the domestic brands of Ferrari and Maserati. The aim was to sell 275 cars there in 2007, up from 150 in 2006 and just 43 in 2004.

New models were of course in the pipeline, and on 19 July 2007 the last Vanquish S rolled out of the Newport Pagnell factory. This was also intended to be the last car made there (although that part of the plan would eventually be subverted), and work now began on converting the

ALONGSIDE THE VANQUISH AND THE DB9

The complexity of the Aston Martin model range has rarely been easy to grasp, and it is important to bear in mind that the Vanquish and the DB9 were not the only models in production between 2001 (when the Vanquish was launched) and 2016 (when the last DB9 was made). The following are the models that completed the Aston Martin product portfolio in those years.

DB7 V12 **1997–2003**
The V12-engined version of the 1993 DB7 was still in production when the Vanquish was launched in 2001.

V8 Vantage **2005–2018**
This more compact Aston was priced below the DB9 but was also deliberately more sporting and less GT. The 380bhp 4.3-litre V8 engine was derived from a Jaguar unit, and from 2008 had 4.7 litres and 420bhp. A Roadster variant arrived in 2009, and a 430bhp Vantage S in 2011. The Vantage went on to become Aston's best-selling model ever.

DBS **2007–2012**
The DBS replaced the Vanquish as the Aston Martin flagship, powered by a 510bhp version of the V12 engine. The car was derived from the DB9 but had more aggressive styling and was less forgiving to drive. It was accompanied by a Volante version from 2009.

V12 Vantage **2009–2018**
The V12 was the smaller Vantage model, with a 510bhp V12 engine instead of the original V8. A Roadster model arrived in 2012, and a 565bhp Vantage S in 2013. A top speed of 330km/h (205mph) made this the fastest production Aston Martin yet.

Rapide **2009–2012**
This model explored the market for a four-door saloon badged as an Aston Martin, but was less successful than hoped. It was a 296km/h (184mph) car with the V12 engine in 470bhp form.

One-77 **2010–2012**
This hand-built, cost-no-object hypercar was limited to 77 examples (hence the name) and had a 750bhp V12 engine of 7.3 litres. It was priced at £1.15 million and could exceed 354km/h (220mph).

Cygnet **2010–2013**
The Cygnet was essentially a Toyota IQ city car reworked by Aston Martin and with a price tag to match. There were hopes that Aston buyers would take one to provide a runabout alongside their proper Aston Martin, but only a few hundred were sold. In the end, it was always a 1330cc Toyota with 97bhp.

Virage **2011–2012**
This model was designed to fit into the range between the DB9 and the DBS, with a 490bhp version of the V12 engine. Sales were slow, though. There is more about the Virage in Chapter 8.

Vanquish **2012–2018**
The new flagship model that replaced the DBS took on the name pioneered by the DBS's predecessor. The engine was a 565bhp V12, giving a top speed of 323km/h (201mph). There was a Volante version from late 2013, and a 595bhp Vanquish S arrived in late 2016.

Rapide S **2013–2020**
A major re-work of the earlier Rapide four-door delivered a more aggressive-looking car with a 550bhp V12 engine and 306km/h (190mph) top speed. There was a further series of improvements in late 2014 as Aston tweaked the model to meet expectations.

Lagonda Taraf **2015–2017**
Based on the Rapide S, this 313km/h (195mph) luxury saloon had a longer wheelbase to make it a full four-seater. The Lagonda name had last been used in 1990. The engine was a 540bhp V12, and the price nudged £800,000.

premises at Tickford Street into the Aston Martin Works heritage department. The plan at that stage was to concentrate all future production at the far more modern factory in Gaydon, although by March 2008 Aston Martin had negotiated a partnership with contract manufacturer Magna Steyr at Graz in Austria, where 2,000 cars were expected to be built a year.

The changes came thick and fast. It was also in 2008 that Aston Martin opened a dedicated test centre at the Nürburgring race track in Germany, and in September that year the company announced that it would revive the Lagonda name. Meanwhile, continued expansion saw the recruitment of more dealers in Europe and of the first two in China, where economic growth was opening new opportunities for Western luxury goods. While all this was happening, however, a global economic recession was building, and Aston Martin, no more immune to its effects than any other luxury brand, found itself obliged to cut its workforce from 1,850 to 1,250 by the end of the year.

The difficulties did not end there. In 2007 Aston Martin had sold a healthy 7,300 cars, but sales and profitability now began a downward spiral. Despite its excellence as a product, sales of the DB9 that was central to the range were failing to generate the funds that Aston Martin needed to develop new models. Although the Graz factory had started to produce the new Rapide four-door grand touring model during 2010, in September 2011 Aston Martin announced that production would be transferred to its Gaydon factory in the second half of 2012. This was quite obviously a cost-saving measure, and a clear sign that the production area at Gaydon was not being completely filled by the other Aston Martin models then on sale. By 2012, Aston Martin was in

Reaching for the stars.... Aston Martin's entry into the hypercar market was the One-77, with a top speed in excess of 355km/h (220mph).

The Vantage became Aston's best-selling car ever. Here it is in short-lived V12 Volante form.

need of more funds, and that December the Italian private equity fund Investindustrial bought a 37.5 per cent stake in the company, investing £150 million to increase its capital.

The crunch came in 2013. Chairman Dave Richards went back to Prodrive, and long-standing CEO Ulrich Bez was made non-executive Chairman. In September 2014 Andy Palmer was recruited from Nissan as the new CEO. By that time, annual sales had dropped to a low of 4,200. It was already clear that Aston Martin could not afford to develop another new engine, and in 2013 the company had reached an agreement with Daimler-Benz. That company, which already had a 5 per cent holding in Aston Martin, would increase its stake to 20 per cent. At the same time it agreed to provide Mercedes-AMG engines for the next generation of cars, and to extend its technical partnership to cover electrical systems as well.

The year 2014 saw a pre-tax loss of £72 million, or about three times the 2013 figure, on sales of just 3,500 cars. The company would not return to profit during the lifetime of the DB9, and in 2016, the year when the last DB9 was built, it was reported that Aston Martin's pre-tax losses increased to £162.8 million, or 27 per cent more than the losses for 2015. Fortunately, after six consecutive years of trading losses, the company returned to profit in 2017 with an end-of-year figure of £87 million, as sales began to climb again and the year's total increased to 5,000 cars. These figures were, of course, boosted by new models in the shape of the DBX sport-utility vehicle of 2015 (which would be built in a new factory at St Athan in Wales) and the DB11 replacement for the DB9 that was announced at Geneva in March 2016.

So Aston Martin had experienced another of its periodic crises – and had emerged triumphant once again. As CEO Andy Palmer put it: 'In the first century we went bankrupt seven times. The second century is about making sure that is not the case.'

CHAPTER 2

VANQUISH DESIGN AND DEVELOPMENT

The story of the 21st century Aston Martin really begins in 1998 with the appearance of a stunning concept car at the North American International Auto Show in Detroit in January 1998. Finished in bright metallic Derwent Green, Project Vantage was described as a vision for a future sports coupé, but it was quite clearly much more serious in intent than most of the 'visions' and 'concepts' that car manufacturers produce to draw attention to their stands at motor shows. It looked like a real, viable car that could make production, and its visual relationship to the existing production DB7 coupé left onlookers in little doubt that this was a preview of the next-generation Aston Martin.

Comments attributed to Aston Martin's Chairman and CEO, Bob Dover, only reinforced this impression. He said:

> *Although we have no plans for the production of this technologically advanced Grand Touring car, it has been designed and planned so that it could be constructed individually, employing the traditional skills and craftsmanship for which Aston Martin is world famous. We believe that the Vantage Project reflects all essential elements of power, performance and driver involvement in a manner which is true to the traditions of Aston Martin.*

Production plans or no production plans, it was fairly obvious that the amount of effort that had gone into creating this machine far exceeded what was needed to create a mere concept car to draw people's attention at motor shows.

Project Vantage was technically advanced, too. The press release that accompanied it spoke of a 320km/h (200mph)-plus supercar that was 'the direct result of close and continuing co-operation between engineers and designers at

The cover of the Detroit press pack promised something very interesting indeed for Aston Martin aficionados...

Aston Martin, Ford Advanced Vehicle Technology, Borg Warner, Magneti Marelli, AP Racing, ITT, TWR and other Aston Martin suppliers'. The release went on to say that Project Vantage 'draws heavily on the advanced research programmes currently being conducted by Ford AVT, and the wealth of experience which this group has gained from participation in Formula 1 Grand Prix racing and other areas of international motor sport.'

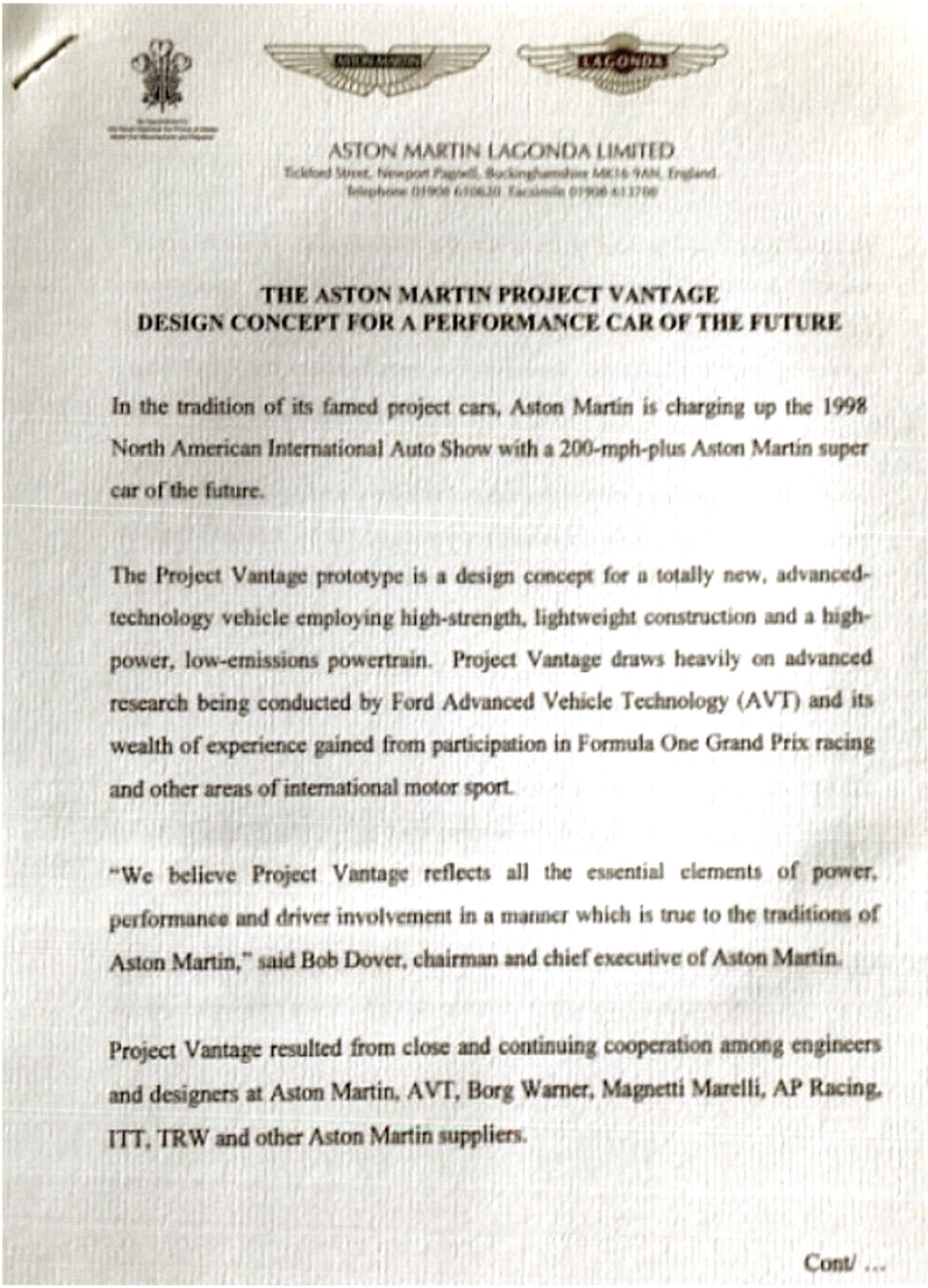

ASTON MARTIN LAGONDA LIMITED
Tickford Street, Newport Pagnell, Buckinghamshire MK16 9AN, England.
Telephone 01908 610620 Facsimile 01908 613708

THE ASTON MARTIN PROJECT VANTAGE
DESIGN CONCEPT FOR A PERFORMANCE CAR OF THE FUTURE

In the tradition of its famed project cars, Aston Martin is charging up the 1998 North American International Auto Show with a 200-mph-plus Aston Martin super car of the future.

The Project Vantage prototype is a design concept for a totally new, advanced-technology vehicle employing high-strength, lightweight construction and a high-power, low-emissions powertrain. Project Vantage draws heavily on advanced research being conducted by Ford Advanced Vehicle Technology (AVT) and its wealth of experience gained from participation in Formula One Grand Prix racing and other areas of international motor sport.

"We believe Project Vantage reflects all the essential elements of power, performance and driver involvement in a manner which is true to the traditions of Aston Martin," said Bob Dover, chairman and chief executive of Aston Martin.

Project Vantage resulted from close and continuing cooperation among engineers and designers at Aston Martin, AVT, Borg Warner, Magnetti Marelli, AP Racing, ITT, TRW and other Aston Martin suppliers.

Cont/ ...

... and the contents were certainly exciting.

Low, sleek, and finished in a very British metallic green, Project Vantage made a stunning statement of intent when it appeared at the Detroit show in 1998.

Ian Callum's body design contained echoes of earlier Aston Martin models, and could not have been mistaken for any other make of car.

Most striking from this angle were the 'haunches' that gave such an appearance of latent power to the concept car. They were a modern interpretation of those on the Zagato-designed DB4GT.

Exactly when Project Vantage was initiated remains unclear to this day, but it seems fairly clear that it was the result of some Ford strategic thinking in the mid-1990s. Aston Martin was ticking over quite nicely with strong sales of the DB7 and reasonable sales of its more expensive Vantage flagship, but if it was to attain the place on the international automotive stage that Ford wanted for it, the company needed not just new products but cutting-edge new products that would attract a wider audience. The company itself simply did not have the resources to create such products – but the vast Ford empire did. What was also then gradually becoming clear within Ford, although not yet to the wider world, was that Aston Martin was the ideal marque to take on a new role as the early adopter of new technologies within the Ford group world wide.

STYLING BY CALLUM

It had made good sense to farm out the styling aspects of the project to TWR Design at Kidlington in Oxfordshire, whose Chief Designer Ian Callum had also designed the DB7. Aston Martin still had no full-time styling department of its own, and for a company that introduced new models fairly rarely, that should come as no surprise. TWR Design was an offshoot of Tom Walkinshaw Racing, and Callum, like the forceful Tom Walkinshaw himself, was a Scotsman. There was no mistaking the family resemblance between Callum's two designs, but Project Vantage was distinctly more aggressive than the almost delicate DB7. To use a word popular in the business environment of the time, it was an uncompromising design. Many years later, Callum would recall that 'It was one of the nicest projects I've ever worked on.'

The two major influences on the styling of Project Vantage were Ian Callum's own DB7 design, and the Zagato-bodied DB4GT of the early 1960s. From the Zagato car came the powerful rear wings, reminiscent of an animal crouched ready to pounce, and the front-wing air vents with their distinctive single bright strake. The curvaceous and sleek front end broadly followed the lines of the DB7, with a series of compound curves that swept back to meet the similarly curvaceous cab superstructure, and the car's low stance on its multi-spoke alloy wheels left a powerful impression. The tail details, too, were reminiscent of the DB7.

The characteristically Aston Martin-shaped grille and lower air intake were flanked by driving lamps and turn indicators, while large clear glass covers over the high-tech headlamps blended into the shapes of the wings. The headlamps themselves were four 25,000-volt high-intensity discharge units that delivered twice the output of conventional halogen headlamps to give a spread of light appropriate to a car of this performance potential. As for the metallic green paint, it hinted at the classic Aston racing colour of the early 1960s, although it was in practice far more arresting to suit the show-car ethos.

Callum's small team at TWR was also responsible for the interior design, which had more of the air of a typical show car, with large areas of structural extruded aluminium on display, and a somewhat awkward (if attention-grabbing)

Mounted on slave wheels, this was the styling buck for the Project Vantage car.

The concept car was of course built with left-hand drive to add appeal for its American audience, and the eventual production models would stay remarkably true to Ian Callum's ideas.

carbon-fibre peak over the major dials. Everything seemed designed to be functional, and there was no suggestion that this might become anything other than a two-seater coupé. Its two seats were carefully shaped to give maximum support to their occupants, and each had a four-point safety harness to reinforce the car's racing heritage. The rest of the interior had what the Detroit press release called 'an imaginative combination of traditional Connolly hide and suede upholstery matched to brushed aluminium and carbon fibre for many of the interior surfaces.' There was even matching tailored luggage fitted in the boot and the interior lockers.

The visible structural elements in the cabin were perhaps deliberately intended to draw attention to the advanced structure of the Project Vantage car, and it was here that Aston Martin broke new ground. The company's cars had depended on separate body and chassis construction since time immemorial, and the existing Vantage flagship model still used it. Only the DB7 showed any acceptance of more modern design trends in its steel monocoque. Yet the structure that had been devised for Project Vantage was different yet again, and represented a giant step into the future for Aston Martin.

The interior of Project Vantage was a little too avant-garde for some tastes, but such things were to be expected of a concept car intended for motor shows.

The DB4GT Zagato of 1960–1963 was an important influence on the styling of the Project Vantage concept car.

Most importantly perhaps, Project Vantage picked up on the lines that Ian Callum had created for the Aston Martin DB7, so providing a sense of styling continuity. This one is a V12-engined DB7 Vantage coupé.

IAN CALLUM

The man responsible for the overall shape of Project Vantage was born in Scotland in 1954. After studying in Coventry, Aberdeen and Glasgow, he graduated from the Royal College of Art in London with a Master's Degree in Vehicle Design.

Between 1979 and 1990, Callum worked for Ford in Britain, Japan, Italy and Australia, and was subsequently appointed Design Manager for the Ghia Design Studio in Turin. Here he worked on several show-car concepts before leaving to join Peter Stevens and Tom Walkinshaw to form TWR Design in 1991.

It was as Chief Designer and General Manager of TWR Design that he first became involved with Aston Martin. The TWR studio worked on concepts for several other manufacturers, and Callum was also involved with designs for Volvo and Mazda, as well as Nissan, for whom he designed the R390 Le Mans 24 Hours racer in the late 1990s.

In 1999, Callum was appointed as Design Director of Jaguar to succeed the late Geoff Lawson. Jaguar and Aston Martin both belonged to Ford at the time, and for a couple of years Callum oversaw design for both marques. It was during this period that he designed both the V8 Vantage and the DB9, the former actually being done first, although it would follow the DB9 into production. From 2001, he was able to devote his attention full-time to Jaguar, when Henrik Fisker was appointed as the dedicated Aston Martin Design Director.

Ian Callum remained Jaguar's Director of Design until summer 2019, and was appointed a CBE (Commander of the Order of the British Empire) for services to the British car industry in the Queen's Birthday Honours that June. He remained a consultant for the Jaguar brand, but also founded his own automotive and product design agency in Warwick, with the simple name of Callum.

Ian Callum drew up the shape of the Aston Martin V12 Vanquish during his time at TWR. He later became the Design Director for Jaguar.

AN INNOVATIVE STRUCTURE

Uncredited in that list of contributors in the Detroit press release, the British firm of Lotus had nevertheless played a quite major role in creating the new Project Vantage structure. Lotus Engineering was an offshoot of the famous car manufacturer that provided a comprehensive range of technical services to many larger automotive companies, and they had taken the lead in designing and developing a massively strong body that drew on aerospace construction techniques to deliver a strong and torsionally rigid platform without incurring major weight penalties. It was made entirely of carbon fibre and aluminium, with its component elements joined by the latest bonding processes. The Detroit press release spoke of a structure that provided 'all the engineering efficiencies, structural integrity, torsional rigidity and occupant protection of a modern Formula 1 car.'

Central to the whole body structure was a carbon-fibre backbone. The floor and the front and rear bulkheads were formed from extruded aluminium sections that were bonded and riveted around this central backbone. The single-piece advanced glass composite inner body side sections were created by having the glass strands chopped and sprayed by robot into the mould, so offering excellent control of thickness and strength. Carbon-fibre windscreen pillars with a revolutionary structure of plaited carbon fibres wound around a foam core were then bonded to the central

The advanced composite construction of the Vanquish body was developed in conjunction with Lotus Engineering. This cutaway shows the essential features of the production design.

Aston Martin produced this cutaway drawing to give further insight into the composite construction of the Vanquish body.

structure, and the entire roof structure was made of double-skinned carbon fibre. The result was an enormously strong safety cell. Bolt-on front and rear structures incorporating complex aluminium castings and carbon-fibre crash members then created energy-absorbing crush zones, while two sub-frames carried the front suspension plus engine and the rear suspension.

All this advanced new technology was concealed under hand-finished, superformed aluminium panels that presented the lines of Ian Callum's design. Superforming was a new metal-shaping process in which the material – in this case aluminium – was heated to a soft state and then the die was drawn up from below. It was not quite the hand-wheeling and beating of Aston Martin tradition, but the company would later make a point of retaining its traditional craftsmen to hand-fit the panels to the production cars and bond them to the main body structure.

As compared to the Aston Martin Vantage that was then in production, this new design of body offered a weight saving of more than 50 per cent in tandem with an increase in torsional rigidity of more than 100 per cent. The Detroit press release was also anxious to make the link with Formula 1 technology, and pointed out that a central venturi incorporated in the flat underbody created a positive down force in order to aid directional stability at high speeds.

THE NEW V12 ENGINE

All this was good, attention-grabbing news, but what really captured the imagination of press and public alike was the new V12 engine that powered the car. Previous Astons had had 6 cylinder or V8 engines, and even a supercharged Jaguar powerplant – but this was something new and exciting. The press release described it as 'a prototype 6.0-litre aluminium alloy V12 48-valve engine which is one of the units currently being evaluated by Aston Martin, Ford AVT and Cosworth Engineering of Northampton in a wide ranging study designed to establish and identify Aston Martin's potential engine requirements for the future.'

Ford were understandably keen to point out that the base design came from their Advanced Vehicle Technology (AVT) division, but added that 'this advanced V12 unit is capable of being developed to provide the required levels of performance for the Vantage Project while meeting or exceeding the world's strictest emission standards. For example, its high efficiency exhaust system has been designed to incorporate a 9.0-litre catalyst.'

What was not revealed at Detroit in 1998 was the fascinating history of the engine, which could be traced back to the early 1990s. That enthralling-sounding V12 could trace its origins to a 4-valve, 60-degree V6 engine that was designed as a joint project by the two Japanese manufacturers Mazda and Suzuki. The two companies sought design expertise from Porsche in Germany, and the engine was brought to market with several different versions. The one most relevant to this story was the 2.5-litre KL-ZE type, a high-revving, high-compression derivative that had outputs of 198bhp and 165 lb ft. It appeared in some versions of the Mazda MX-6 coupé in 1992, and was sold mainly in Japan.

At this stage, Mazda was partly owned by Ford, and the American company decided to base its second-generation Probe sports coupé on the MX-6. As a result, the 1993-model Probe had a less powerful version of the engine called the KL-DE, with 163bhp and 156lb ft of torque. Meanwhile, Ford had recognised the engine's potential, and took it to Cosworth Engineering in Britain for further development. The result of that was the engine that Ford knew as their Duratec V6, with a 2967cc (nominal 3.0-litre) swept volume.

The Duratec V6 began to appear in Ford products in the USA and in Europe from 1993, and its tuning potential led to it being proposed as a future engine for Jaguar, which company was, of course, also owned by Ford at the time. However, Jaguar decided against using it in its forthcoming F-type sports model. Meanwhile, an idea originated within Ford's Advanced Vehicle Technology group in the USA, the organisation responsible for generating new technologies for future production vehicles, of developing a 6.0-litre V12 by mounting a pair of 3.0-litre Duratec V6 engines end to end.

There was a lot more to the job than that description suggests, but the idea was taken on by the Core & Advanced Powertrain Engineering team, and within eighteen months of the idea becoming a project a first engine was on dyno test. This was in September 1995, and in the meantime Cosworth Engineering had become involved once again. A programme there saw the cylinder block and cylinder heads being freshly designed around the architecture and dimensions of the Duratec engine. The main journals were also enlarged slightly, and the crankshaft was redesigned, the production version giving uneven firing intervals.

The new V12 engine had not been developed with any production car projects in mind, but more as a speculative venture that might eventually find a home somewhere within the Ford empire. It was ready and running at just the right time to be picked up as the powerplant of a concept car that

THE FORD INDIGO, 1996

The Ford Indigo concept car was developed by Ford in the USA to showcase the company's Indy car-racing technologies on the 1996 motor-show circuit. Just two examples were built, of which only one actually had the new V12 engine.

The 1996 Ford Indigo concept really did have an early version of the V12 engine, but its main purpose was to promote other aspects of the Ford business.

The car was designed as a wedge-shaped two-seater with the overall appearance of an Indy racer and incorporated attention-grabbing features such as scissor-type doors. Its monocoque chassis was developed in conjunction with Reynard Motorsport as a single-piece tub made of a carbon-fibre composite material, while the suspension was essentially the same as that used in Reynard's various Indy cars.

The engineless car was later sold on, but the one built with an engine remained in Ford ownership.

was being prepared for the 1996 US motor show circuit, and which emerged as the Ford Indigo.

Even though the Indigo had a rather different purpose of its own (see the sidebar), the Ford people were clearly very proud of its new engine. A press release of the time claimed that it delivered 435bhp at 6,100rpm with 405lb ft (549Nm) of torque at 5,250rpm, and that it 'represents not only a very powerful engine but also a breakthrough in development cost and timing. This is largely the result of the unit's clever use of existing Ford engine components.'

The release went on to explain that the V12 was based on the 3.0-litre Duratec V6 then used in the Ford Taurus and Mercury Sable:

> *It uses the same bore and stroke dimensions (89.0 x 79.5mm) as the Duratec, and also shares its pistons, rings, rods, valves, valve seals, valve springs and retainers.*
>
> *However, the V-12 block and cylinder heads are all new, cast from 356-T6 aluminium alloy by Cosworth in Great Britain. The cylinder heads retain the Duratec's combustion chamber and exhaust port design. The intake ports incorporate a new, 'tumble-port' design that creates low-rpm, intake-charge turbulence without the need for throttling one of each pair of intake valves.*
>
> *Unlike the Duratec, the V-12 block is not a girdled design. Instead it is deep skirted for extra torsional stiffness. (The V-12 approximates the torsional rigidity of the Duratec V-6 despite its extra length.) The crankshaft is formed using an all-new casting process called 'electro-slag casting', which is claimed to result in crankshafts that are 10 per cent stronger than forged units.*

Five of these original V12s were commissioned from Cosworth, and all of them were retained by Ford after the show season was over. It must have been at about this time that the need for a new Aston Martin engine became apparent, and it was probably a Ford product planner who suggested that the all-alloy V12 was exactly what was needed. The engine was duly handed over to Aston Martin engineers to develop further as they saw fit, and by the time of its

THE LAGONDA RAPIDE CONCEPT, 1993

In the early 1990s, Aston Martin's owners at Ford decided to investigate a revival of the dormant Lagonda brand, which had been acquired by Sir David Brown and merged with Aston Martin in 1947. As part of this investigation, they arranged for a four-door saloon concept car to be built for the 1993 Geneva Motor Show, where it was shown alongside the DB7.

The 1993 Lagonda Vignale concept was planned to have a V12 engine, but none of the examples built actually did. Seen with it are Moray Callum, David Wilkie and Sally Ericson.

The car never went into production because Ford decided that the Lagonda brand was not well enough known outside the UK to justify the cost of reviving it. Its interest to the story of the New Era Aston Martins is that publicity suggested a production version would have a 5935cc 48-valve V12 engine. Those were the specifications of the eventual Aston Martin V12, which at this stage did not exist.

Ford used all the prestigious labels it could find in labelling this car, which was officially an Aston Martin Lagonda Vignale. Ford had owned the rights to the Vignale and Ghia names since 1972, and maintained a design studio under the Ghia name. At that time, Moray Callum, the younger brother of the Ian Callum responsible for the Aston Martin DB7 and the Project Vantage concept, was working at Ghia, and it was he who led design of the Lagonda concept. Its interior design was by David Wilkie, and Sally Ericson did the colour and materials work.

Three of these cars were built. The first two were built by Ghia, and were based on an extended 1990 Lincoln Town Car platform and had that car's 190bhp 4.6-litre Ford V8 engine. One was grey and the other blue; the grey car was destroyed, but the blue car was auctioned off to a collector in 2002. The third car was a more serious investigation of production possibilities and was built by the Aston Martin Works Service department on a different Ford platform; it had a Jaguar V12 engine and other changes from the two Ghia cars. This one was sold to the Sultan of Brunei in 1995.

announcement at Detroit in 1998, it had ceased to be a Ford bright idea and had become a fully fledged Aston Martin powerplant. When the engine entered production in 2003, it became known as the AM04 type, the 04 indicating the model-year for which it was introduced.

GO AND STOP

The press release for Project Vantage at Detroit said that initial calculations had suggested the car would accelerate from rest to 60mph in just 4.0sec, reach more than 225km/h (140mph) at the end of a standing quarter-mile, and still return fuel economy better than 3km (20 miles) to a US gallon. As the US gallon is smaller than the imperial gallon used in the UK, this suggested anything up to about 11.8ltr/100km (24mpg) to a UK audience.

The V12 engine transmitted its power to the rear wheels through a six-speed gearbox that could be used in fully automatic mode or controlled manually through a system of Formula 1-style paddles on the steering wheel that allowed finger-tip control. The gearbox actually in the car had probably come from Borg Warner, whose name appeared in the credits at Detroit (whereas the name of ZF, who would make the eventual production gearboxes, did not).

The Project Vantage prototype also featured a new suspension system, which Ford claimed had benefited from AVT's direct involvement with the Stewart Formula 1 Grand Prix team and the Bridgestone Tyre Project. Be that as it may (and of course the Detroit press release was a great opportunity to drop a few important names), there were wishbones at all four corners of the car. Those at the front were of unequal length and those at the rear were of equal length. There were horizontally located, pushrod-operated spring and damper units, and actively controlled anti-roll bars front and rear. Then to ensure adequate stopping power, the brakes were of AP Racing manufacture, with six-pot aluminium alloy callipers that featured titanium bridge bolts and fittings. These acted on ventilated and drilled discs, with a 15in diameter for the front wheels and a 14in diameter at the rear.

As for the wheels, these had a 19in diameter both front and rear, with 9.5in wide rims. They were cast from lightweight magnesium and wore Bridgestone tyres with an intermediate rubber compound. Those at the front were a 255 x 40 ZR 19 size, while the rears were wider, as was very much the custom on high-performance cars at the time, and had a 285 x 40 ZR 19 size.

THE RUMOUR MILL

By the end of the 1990s, the V12 engine had entered production for the DB7 Vantage and was widely understood to be the engine around which all new Aston Martin models were to be based for the foreseeable future. It was of course essentially a hand-built engine, which gave it a certain cachet, and the relatively slow speed and high cost of its production were as good as a guarantee that Ford would not put it into another model from what had by now become its Premier Automotive Group of companies.

None of that, however, prevented press speculation in 2000 and 2001 that it would be used in the flagship versions of the forthcoming new Range Rover. This had originally been planned with a BMW V12 engine before Land Rover was sold to Ford's PAG in 2000, and there was no obvious V12 in the Ford stable to replace the BMW engine. In fact the speculation was simply that, and the idea of using the Aston Martin V12 was never seriously contemplated because the engine could not have been built in the volumes that such a project would have needed.

THE ASTON MARTIN VANQUISH

The very positive reactions to Project Vantage at the Detroit motor show undoubtedly confirmed whatever plans Ford had already devised for Aston Martin to put the car into production. The reality was probably that Detroit was treated as a sanity check: if there had been an adverse reaction for some reason, no doubt a rethink would have followed, but all the signs were good. The new Aston project went ahead with all speed in the aftermath of the show.

Much of the important work had already been done, and that enabled Ford to set an initial target of autumn 2000 for the global introduction of the new car. This was around two and a half years away – a time-frame unthinkable if the concept car had not been conceived as a prototype as well as a show special. At Newport Pagnell, Ian Minards was appointed the Project Director for what was to be named the Aston Martin Vanquish (exactly when the name was chosen is not clear), and visually, the production car would remain remarkably faithful to Ian Callum's original design.

WHAT HAPPENED TO THE PROJECT VANTAGE PROTOTYPE?

After its introduction at the Detroit show in January 1998, the Project Vantage prototype was shown on the concept lawn at the Pebble Beach concours in August. Back in the UK, it was displayed at the exclusive Hurlingham Club and again as a static exhibit at the Aston Martin Owners' Club race meeting at Donington Park in October. It then disappeared from public view for more than five years.

From autumn 2003, the car was displayed in the reception area of the Aston Martin Works Service department at Newport Pagnell alongside a production V12 Vanquish. It was otherwise seen in public only once, at the Vanquish Day celebration event held at Aston Martin Works in 2014.

Like many earlier Aston Martin prototypes, this show car was actually fully engineered and was quite capable of running on the road. Nevertheless, when the company decided to offer it for sale through Bonhams auctioneers in 2016, they pointed out that it could not be registered for road use and was therefore offered for display or track day use only. 'Aston Martin inform us that this vehicle is not fully functioning, but is a concept car designed to motivate itself at slow speeds,' they added.

At auction on 21 May 2016, the car fetched £87,740 including the buyer's premium. At the time, a standard production Vanquish, by then between nine and fifteen years old, could be had for upwards of about £60,000.

There were some changes, of course, and most of them were made out of a need for greater practicality. The production Vanquish would be slightly taller than the concept – all of 10mm (0.8in) in fact – and the car would appear rather less hunkered down over its wheels, although only a careful comparison would reveal the difference. Turn signals were added within the auxiliary light apertures in the front apron, as were repeater indicators on the front wings. The mesh in the lower air intake disappeared, the door mirrors were changed, and the headlamps were changed for pairs of projector lamps without altering the long glass fairings that gave the front of the car so much of its character.

Putting that revolutionary new body structure into production was of course a separate headache. It was a huge leap for Aston Martin at the time, requiring complex new manufacturing processes that demanded a precision only achievable through computer control. Aston Martin had never even attempted to build anything like it, and it was here that the vast resources of parent Ford came into play. A separate but related programme dealt with these complexities, and the manufacturing processes were developed both at the University of Nottingham in the UK and at Cupertino, in northern California's Silicon Valley.

Within the Aston Martin engineering department, the 6.0-litre V12 engine was further developed for its new role. At the time when Project Vantage was shown in Detroit, the V12 was still just an advanced engineering concept, but within a year it had been developed for production and would be announced in March 1999 as the powerplant of the DB7 Vantage, with a 420bhp output. For the Vanquish, further development would focus on reducing weight and increasing power. The existing torque of 400lb ft at 5,000rpm was considered adequate and in fact remained unchanged for the Vanquish version of the engine.

The new engine ended up some 18kg (40lb) lighter than the DB7 version, more than half of that weight being saved by removing metal from the flywheel and the crankshaft. Different material used for the new crankshaft actually made it stronger than before, and this, in tandem with a lightened valve train, allowed the engine to rev higher than before. A new induction system was designed, the compression ratio was slightly raised, and the camshafts were reworked. The catalytic converters were now close coupled to the two cylinder banks, and on the production cars would have chimney-like ducts that carried their waste heat to twin outlets near the back of the bonnet – a system found necessary to prevent the composite materials used in the body structure being affected by the heat from the engine's six separate catalytic converters. The exhaust system was also fitted with special valving to control back pressure.

The original Borg Warner automatic gearbox became a casualty of the development programme, but the Aston Martin engineers did manage to retain the F1-style paddle shifts of the concept car and also a two-pedal control system. They achieved what they wanted by starting with a six-speed manual gearbox made by ZF in Germany. To this they added an electronic control system made by Magneti Marelli that was designed to work with the paddle shifts. Although the system depended on a conventional clutch, this was hydraulically operated by servo motors actuated by the electronic control system. A further refinement designed into the system was a fully automatic mode, so that the driver could choose whether to drive the car as an automatic or a paddle-shift manual.

The V12 Vanquish would be assembled in the Newport Pagnell factory that had seen the birth of so many legendary Aston Martin models since the mid-1950s.

The paddle shifts were later claimed to give exceptionally fast gearchanges of as little as a third of a second, and the system automatically blipped the throttle on downshifts to ensure a smooth take-up of the drive. It would prove to be a system that took some learning, and not everyone who drove the production V12 liked it, or mastered it, which led to complaints of slow gearshifts. A further control was a 'Sport' button on the dashboard that was arranged to give the faster shifts its name suggested, and there was a 'Winter' button as well to reduce engine output and avoid wheelspin on snowy or icy surfaces.

More work had to be done on the interior of the passenger cabin, where the concept-car elements had to be toned down to produce a design that would be more generally acceptable. The designers aimed for less aluminium and more leather, although some of the aluminium elements were retained as a demonstration of modernity; at this stage in the development of the Vanquish, the plan was to avoid traditional wood trim altogether.

Some of the aluminium elements ended up being replaced by aluminium-look plastic. Others disappeared behind more conventional trim, and the awkward carbon-fibre cowl over the instrument panel gave way to a more conventional-looking trimmed cowl that blended smoothly into the contours of the facia. The handbrake moved from the transmission tunnel to a position alongside the driver's seat, and a rather more conventional-looking airbag steering wheel was designed. Nevertheless, the production version that emerged at the end of the process was still a close relative of the interior in the concept car, and most notably the sweeping dashboard centre stack was still a dominant feature, even if it was no longer quite as demanding of attention as it had been.

VANQUISH PROTOTYPES

The Vanquish incorporated so much technology that was new to Aston Martin that it was necessary to test it in an unusually large number of prototypes. Some of the early ones were strictly 'mules', with drivetrain and perhaps suspension elements built into the modified bodyshells of other Ford products. There are exclusive and fascinating pictures of some of these on the astonmartins.com web site that is run by Tim Cottingham (note that the similarly named www.astonmartin.com – without the 's' – is the official web site of the company, and not the same thing at all).

Aston Martin never commented on rumours that the development costs had been far greater than the original budget, but they did say at the launch of the Vanquish that they had built 50 prototypes in all – an unprecedented quantity for the company. These were tested world-wide, and as examples the company cited hot-weather testing in Australia and cold-weather testing in Canada. Aston Martin engineers had worked with Lotus Engineering again to fine-tune the chassis, and there had been input from Ford engineers as well, supposedly including the company's highly regarded suspension guru, Richard Parry-Jones. The test cars had covered over a million miles to prove the durability of the components and to ensure that the production cars would deliver a driving experience that was fully in keeping with customer expectations of the Aston Martin brand.

Despite the modern composite structure, there was plenty of traditional hand assembly work on the Vanquish at Newport Pagnell.

Each body passed through the assembly process mounted on its own individual trolley, as seen here.

The end of the assembly line is seen here, with completed examples of the Vanquish awaiting final preparation and sign-off. Dark metallic grey was a popular colour!

TECHNICAL SPECIFICATIONS: PROJECT VANTAGE

Engine
V12 with 4 valves per cylinder
5935cc (89mm bore x 79.5 stroke)
450bhp at 6,000rpm

Gearbox
Six-speed Borg Warner automatic with paddle-shift manual over-ride control.

Suspension
Front suspension with unequal-length wishbones, coil springs, and actively controlled anti-roll bar.

Rear suspension with equal-length wishbones, coil springs, and actively controlled anti-roll bar.

Steering
Rack-and-pinion system with power assistance.

Brakes
AP Racing six-piston callipers front and rear, acting on ventilated and drilled discs with a 15in (380mm) diameter at the front and a 14in (355mm) diameter at the rear; ABS.

Wheels and tyres
19in (483mm) cast magnesium wheels with 9.5in (241mm) rims. Bridgestone 255/40ZR19 tyres (front) and 275/40ZR19 tyres (rear).

Dimensions

Overall length:	4,666mm (183.7in)
Overall width:	1,890mm (74.4in)
Overall height:	1,298mm (51.1in)
Wheelbase:	2,692mm (106in)
Track, front:	1,549mm (61in)
Track, rear:	1,600mm (63in)

Weight
1,550kg (3,417lb)

CHAPTER 3

THE V12 VANQUISH, 2001–2004

The original plan was for the Vanquish to be given its worldwide introduction at the British International Motor Show in October 2000, but when Dr Ulrich Bez arrived as Aston Martin's new CEO in July, he put things on hold. Bez was not at all happy about the interior design and held out for some changes to be made. He was not wrong to do so: even after the changes had been made, there would be some quite strong criticism in the media of the car's interior.

The launch was rescheduled to take place at the Geneva Show that opened on 27 February 2001. In the meantime, a pre-production Vanquish was shown to groups of potential customers and selected media representatives in October 2000 to drum up some pre-launch enthusiasm. Production at Newport Pagnell was geared for a start to deliveries in spring 2001.

The official line was that Bez had called for some alterations to the interior that would allow more scope for wood and carbon-fibre trims alongside the aluminium ones always planned, and to allow for different types of upholstery with both leather and cloth. That may in itself have been true, and there was no doubt that the option of customisation was a vital one for the Aston Martin brand. However, it appears

Several early examples of the Vanquish used for publicity and on the press launch were registered in the Y-MWL sequence. As this picture shows, these good-looking cars embodied a sense of power.

that a much bigger concern was how many interior items Aston Martin had borrowed from cars already in production by other members of the Ford group.

Jaguar was a primary source, and had provided the controls planned for the climate control and sound systems, as well as the door handles and window switches. It is said that the air vents had come directly from the Ford Ka – a quirky low-cost city car intended for European and Latin American markets. Bez set the Aston Martin team to work on disguising the origins of those items, which had to be retained for cost reasons, though the Ford Ka air vents were thrown out and replaced by slightly more up-market ones from the Volvo division of the Premier Automotive Group.

Thus reworked, the Vanquish made its bow at Geneva to a very enthusiastic reception. The official line was cautious in the beginning, suggesting that the car would be built at a rate of 300 a year, but customer response was immediate and overwhelmingly positive. By August 2001, *Autocar* magazine was able to report that 'all 500 to be built this year have already found homes and the waiting list stretches through 2003.' Around 30 per cent of all those built were expected to be sold in the USA, which was of course a major market for Aston Martin.

WHAT'S IN A NAME?

The Aston Martin that was derived from the 1998 Project Vantage and was built between 2001 and 2007 was always known as the V12 Vanquish. This name distinguishes it from the later Vanquish, the VH310 model built from 2012, which of course also had a V12 engine. The Vanquish name had not been used for a production Aston Martin before 2001.

THE FIRST CARS

In Britain, the launch price was £158,000, but it was not difficult to increase that by adding such items as satellite navigation (£2,109). In the USA, the list price in autumn 2002 was $225,000, and of course similar considerations about extras and options applied. All the cars would be coupés – there are no indications that an open Volante derivative of the Vanquish was ever considered – and the standard interior configuration consisted of just two seats with a luggage platform behind them. At extra cost – about £6,000 in Britain – the car could be configured as a 2+2 with fully upholstered rear seats, which were, in truth, 'not really fit for human occupation' in the words of an *Autocar* road test from August 2001.

It would have been hard to be disappointed with one of these early V12 Vanquish models, although those who were so minded could point to the fact that the production cars did not quite live up to the performance anticipated back in 1998 for the Project Vantage concept. The 0–60mph acceleration time of 4.6sec was a little slower than the predicted 4.0sec, and the top speed of 306km/h (190mph) was not the 320km/h (200mph) that had seized imaginations three years earlier. Nevertheless, this was unmistakeably a credible challenger for the Ferrari and Porsche models that were then the benchmarks in the performance GT class.

Right from the start, Aston Martin recognised that some customers would have trouble becoming acclimatised to the paddle-shift gearbox. So a day's one-to-one tuition on the company's Performance Driving Course was included in the price of the car, and was offered to every new V12 Vanquish owner. While most buyers who accepted probably focused on the idea of learning to drive their new high-performance cars safely and effectively, they were also shown how to get the best out of the new control system so they would not complain about it later! Though inevitably some did, of course.

There were plenty of other systems to get used to in driving the car, and those who just got in and drove without reading the manual would probably have had quite a few surprises in the early days of ownership. There was, of course, no spare wheel, but just an emergency puncture

The single strake on the mesh air grille extended on to the leading edge of each door.

A Vanquish and the road ahead.... here the location of the high-mounted third brake light at the bottom of the rear window is clear to see.

Standard wheels on the early Vanquish were the attractive twelve-spokes. The design was perhaps unexceptional in itself, but suited the car very well. The cross-drilled brake disc and red enamelled calliper are visible through the spokes.

The twin headlights were concealed under a sleek, transparent fairing that allowed them to blend with the lines of the wing.

kit; this was an increasingly common trend at the time, not least to reduce costs but also to save space and weight as cars became more and more complex. The Yokohama AVS road tyres all had a 40-section profile, but the rear pair were wider than the fronts (285/40 and 255/40 respectively) in order to optimise handling. The rear pair also had a bespoke rubber compound that was unique to Aston Martin, and to advertise this fact they had Aston Martin winged logos moulded on to their sidewalls. To reduce the risk of a driver not noticing that a tyre was losing air, the cars all came with a tyre-pressure warning system as standard.

The 19in wheels, meanwhile, had a simple but stylish twelve-spoke design, through which it was possible to see the huge cross-drilled and ventilated brake discs with their bright red callipers that carried the Aston Martin name. A Teves ABS system was standard, a traction control system acted on both throttle and brakes to help the car maintain serene progress, and of course there was also a limited-slip differential to maintain a degree of control if the driver became a little too enthusiastic.

BUILDING THE VANQUISH

The V12 Vanquish replaced the Virage on the assembly lines at Aston Martin's Newport Pagnell factory, joining the range alongside the DB7 that was built in larger numbers in the much more modern factory at Bloxham in Oxfordshire. This was perhaps not an ideal arrangement for a car that depended on so much new technology, for the Newport Pagnell factory was very much an old-style car assembly plant. Nevertheless, Aston Martin were prepared to work within its limitations. The V12 Vanquish was the company's flagship model, and it was not likely to sell in the same high numbers as the DB7, so production volumes did not need to be as high.

Newport Pagnell was designated as the assembly plant for the V12 Vanquish, but of course not every element of manufacture was carried out there. The V12 engines, for example, were assembled by Cosworth Engineering in Northampton before being delivered to Aston Martin. The complex body unit came from Hydro Automotive Structures in Worcester, who delivered the bare shells to Newport Pagnell.

It was at Newport Pagnell that the hand-building that had always been such an important part of the Aston Martin ethos now came into the picture. Aston Martin were determined that there should remain a genuine element of hand-finishing in the V12 Vanquish, and the craftsmen who had hand-finished the panels of earlier Aston Martin models at Newport Pagnell were retained for the important job of fitting and fettling the new superformed skin panels of the Vanquish.

All this hand-finishing of course added considerably to the build time of a V12 Vanquish. That may have been a drawback, but there was more than adequate compensation in the retention of a 'traditional' aura for the Aston Martin brand, and in the superb levels of fit and finish that could be achieved on the cars that came out of Newport Pagnell.

WHAT THE PRESS THOUGHT

Not every motoring magazine was granted the privilege of testing Aston Martin's latest car, and the small Vanquish test fleet was lent out sparingly in the UK. Nevertheless, there were enough evaluations and road tests published in the early days to leave a lasting record of how the car appeared at the time. The extracts chosen here are intended to give the flavour of media reactions, and are taken from three printed reports. Two come from British magazines, *Autocar* of 8 August 2001 and *Top Gear* dated September 2001, and the third comes from the American magazine *Road & Track* of September 2002.

'Conceptually and technologically [the Vanquish] is the biggest step forward Aston has taken since the introduction of the DB4 in 1959,' said *Autocar.* The car was also solidly and extremely well built, and the lack of squeaks and rattles persuaded the writer of the *Top Gear* report to put it in 'an altogether different league from any Aston I've driven previously. This was,' he summarised, 'a most refined, relaxed and civilised Grand Tourer.'

The American reaction was also very positive. The Vanquish was 'the ultimate Gran Turismo that delivers not only top-notch styling, performance and luxury, but most important, an exhilarating driving experience that excites our senses of sight, sound, smell and touch, all at the same time.' The car's 'powerful presence, its first-rate handling dynamics and fabulously furnished cockpit make for a driving experience unlike any other,' and 'winding along mountain roads, the Vanquish is the perfect companion.'

There was not much to be said about the visual appearance of the car that had not already been said. *Car* magazine had pointed out in its initial evaluation of November 2000 that 'the whole language of the surfaces is stronger

The production interior was dominated by the centre stack with its metallic finish. The instrument panel was now much better integrated into the dash than in the concept car.

Different colours and finishes could produce a very different interior ambience – in this case, sporty and functional rather than overtly luxurious.

[than DB7], more forceful in its visual message, although it's certainly not as brutish as the outgoing V8 series.' However, there were some quite strong opinions about the passenger cabin and the interior design.

Car magazine had established in its early evaluation that the cabin was much more spacious than that of the DB7, and *Autocar* thought that 'the driving position is reasonable, though many will find the steering wheel too far away, despite being both reach and rake adjustable.' *Autocar* also

The wearing surfaces of the seats were diamond quilted, and the wraparound bolsters provided appropriate support.

quibbled with the positioning of the high-level third brake light at the bottom of the rear screen, where they thought it badly restricted visibility. Aston Martin made soothing noises in reply, saying that there were plans to move it to the top of the screen – although in practice that would be some years away.

Autocar was also brutally frank about the details of the interior design (and would probably have been more so before the last-minute changes that Aston's Ulrich Bez had insisted on):

> *'Sadly, the Vanquish's interior is still one we struggle to equate with a car of this price… While individual items look up to snuff in isolation… the overall effect smacks too heavily of parts-bin dependency. Most out of place is the entire centre console, which has been lifted wholesale from Jaguar's XJ saloon – and it didn't look all that great in a car costing less than a quarter of the price of this Aston.*

The *Top Gear* view offered an interesting and more positive counterpoint: 'Finding one's way around the Jaguar-sourced centre console is simple and intuitive.'

Most discussion of the engine focused on the changes that had been made since its appearance in the DB7 Vantage, but *Top Gear* did single out a feature to which Aston Martin had paid special attention:

> *At start-up, and either below 800rpm or above 4,000rpm, a silencer by-pass system operates, so at tickover the Vanquish's chunky twin tailpipes burble beautifully and none too silently. There's an almost pre-war quality to it, not too far removed from the deep, mellow tones emitted by a big old sporting Bentley or Invicta at idle… By contrast, between 800 and 4,000rpm the Vanquish sounds not unlike a big, plush executive saloon from the inside – that is, there is tyre noise but little else.*

There were mixed opinions about the paddle-shift gearbox. 'The entire gearbox installation and application can be described as a success and something approaching a triumph when you consider the 'box started life in a truck,' said *Autocar*. However, they found Aston's claim of lightning-fast

The exposed structural members of the concept car had given way to these grab handles on either side of the transmission tunnel.

Occupants were never allowed to forget what make of car they had the privilege to be in.... note the neatly styled escutcheon for the door release handle and electric window switches.

The paddle-switch controls for the gearbox were mounted behind the steering wheel. This, the right-hand one, changed up, and the other (labelled with a minus sign) changed down.

The personal touch: Vanquish sill plates could be customised like this.

gearshifts to be an overstatement, insisting that the Vanquish had 'a gearchange that *doesn't* swap cogs in less than the blink of an eye', and writing of the 'slight but still irksome pause between upshifts'.

Top Gear was rather more impressed, praising the 'instantaneous downshifts, lightning-quick upshifts, and the ease with which they are accomplished.' They went on to say that 'the paddleshift system really does allow the driver to concentrate fully on the basics of steering, braking and accelerating, while the incidental of gear-ratio choice is dealt with by the simple flick of a finger.' However, 'to extract the most from the system – that is, the smoothest changes in the shortest time – takes a little practice.'

As for *Road & Track*, their view was that 'launching the Vanquish with the paddle-shift transmission is effortless. Leave the car in first gear, step on the throttle and it accelerates rapidly thanks to massive but smooth torque output.' However, excessive enthusiasm was not recommended, as 'aggressive initial throttle input (more than 70 per cent) causes too much wheelspin and hurts acceleration times.'

The steering earned praise from *Autocar*, who wrote of its 'perfectly judged weight', while *Road & Track* in the USA echoed the sentiment and described it as 'nicely weighted'. Opinions of the brakes were more sharply divided, though, and while *Top Gear* said they were 'darn near perfect, with excellent feel and huge power', *Autocar* really slated them. In a car capable of 300km/h (190mph) or more, they 'felt and proved unequal to such performance standards… pedal travel is disconcertingly long, the feel is spongy, and the 0–60mph time of 2.9sec is slower than that of vastly more modest cars.' They concluded that 'the brakes offered, at best, only mediocre performance.'

Both ride and handling qualities were universally judged to be of a high order. The Vanquish was 'the best handling car Aston has ever produced', in the opinion of *Autocar*, and 'rides as well as a DB7. It is firmer, but so fluent is the damping and so well does it maintain its ride height on the most undulating roads that what little (if any) it gives away in secondary absorption, it more than counters with primary body control.' There was nonetheless 'no escaping that the Vanquish is a heavy car', and it could not be flung about willy-nilly. *Road & Track* thought that it 'grips the asphalt with poise', and added that, 'on the road, if the Vanquish's endless pulling power and captivating engine rumble don't impress you, its solid and competent chassis surely will.'

Performance was, of course, considered excellent. *Autocar* thought the claimed 306km/h (190mph) top speed was 'conservative', and suggested in their performance summary table that the maximum in sixth gear would be 315km/h (196mph). At the Bruntingthorpe test track they recorded 4.4sec for the 0–60mph sprint, and took just 10.5sec to reach 160km/h (100mph) from a standing start. This made the Vanquish 'every bit as quick as the Ferrari 550 Maranello (4.6sec/10.1sec) it rivals'. *Top Gear* did not disagree, summarising that, 'there's no doubt that the Vanquish is one very fast car, with the only small chink in its speed portfolio being a slight reluctance to accelerate with real gusto while cruising at normal motorway speeds in sixth.'

There had to be a down side to all this excellence, and there was: *Autocar* recorded an average fuel consumption of just 22ltr/100km (12.6mpg), and complained that the 'awful consumption and small tank seriously compromise range'. Over in the USA, *Road & Track* did surprisingly better on smaller American gallons, recording an overall 21ltr/100km (13.3mpg) for their test, and a cruising range of 430km (267 miles).

LEATHER ORIGINS

Leather upholstery was part of the standard specification for the V12 Vanquish, and the old-established firm of Connolly Brothers proudly supplied the eight hides needed to trim each car. However, Connolly Brothers closed down during 2002, and Aston Martin subsequently obtained their hides from Bridge of Weir, the company that became the new major supplier of upholstery leather to luxury motor manufacturers.

AS DRIVEN BY JAMES BOND

Aston Martin lost no time in improving the image of the Vanquish by getting it featured in a James Bond 007 film that was released in 2002. The film was *Die Another Day*, and the car was heavily featured in it, especially in scenes shot in Iceland, where it was involved in an elaborate chase sequence that included driving on ice. In another useful piece of product placement by Ford, the pursuing car was a high-performance Jaguar XKR.

Although outwardly a standard Vanquish painted in Tungsten Silver, the Bond car followed in the great tradition of 007's Aston Martins by featuring special features supposedly added by Q Branch of Britain's secret service. Alongside the machine guns and missile launchers, tyre spikes for use on snow, and an ejector seat for unwelcome passengers, the major novelty was a 'cloaking device'. This feature led to the car's nickname of 'Vanish', and was based on an idea then under development for military use. This was better known as adaptive camouflage, and allowed the car to blend into its background and so, in effect, to become invisible. Shots of the car's switchgear also suggested that lasers and both mortar and grenade launchers were part of its equipment, though these were not actually used in the film.

There was one more very special feature of the Vanquish used in *Die another Day*: the Vanquish used for filming the snow-and-ice chase was specially equipped with a four-wheel-drive system to improve traction, and had a 300bhp Ford V8 engine as well.

FURTHER CHANGES: THE 2004 MODELS

No doubt the new James Bond film played its part in continuing strong sales for the V12 Vanquish. No important changes were made to the model's specification for the 2003 season, but the 1,000th car was delivered to a customer in Japan in July 2003. The Vanquish had been on sale for just under two years, and that figure made clear why production had been ramped up very early from the 300 a year of the original plan to 500 a year. For Aston Martin, this was success indeed.

More changes were certainly in the pipeline, but for the 2004 season Aston Martin chose to make a few small alterations to the car, and previewed these at the Frankfurt Motor Show in September 2003. The 2004 cars were readily recognisable by their newly designed seven-spoke wheels (although the original twelve-spoke style could still be ordered as an option). The new wheels were 19in in diameter, and were shod with Yokohama tyres, in a 255/40 ZR 19 size at the front and a 285/40 ZR 19 size at the rear. These were accompanied by new Brembo brake discs with

The Vanquish used in the 007 film had a few differences from standard. Here it is at the 2017 Bond in Motion exhibition that was held at the National Film Museum. The Bombardier Ski-Doo also had a role in the film.

This view of two early Vanquish cars from above shows clearly how the passenger cabin tapered towards the rear, emphasising the 'haunches' of the rear wings.

The front end had a blunt and businesslike appearance, and embodied some small changes from the styling of the concept car.

As this early publicity picture of the rear shows, the car was always known as a V12 Vanquish rather than as a Vanquish plain and simple.

competition-derived Pagid friction pads, and the existing ABS system was now supplemented by an EBD (electronic brakeforce distribution) system that achieved even braking when there was a risk that external forces might upset the car's stability.

Newport Pagnell had also taken the opportunity to improve the interior a little, eliminating some of the features that had attracted negative criticism. Perhaps most readily visible was that the bright red starter button in the centre of the dashboard had been replaced by a backlit etched glass button as used in the DB9. (It is said, incidentally, that there was considerable dislike of the original red button within Aston Martin, but that it had been retained in the belief that American customers would like it.) There was also a new 'liquid metal' finish called Platinum for the centre console casting, the instrument pack surround, the door release escutcheons and other minor interior items. New front seats also offered better shoulder support than before.

THE COST WHEN NEW: ASTON MARTIN V12 VANQUISH

These are base prices, without special options and extras.

	UK	*USA*
Vanquish, 2001 (March)	£158,000	
Vanquish, 2001 (later)	£160,000	
Vanquish, 2004	£163,000	
Vanquish, 2005	£163,600	$236,250

THE SPORTS DYNAMIC PACK

Late in 2003, part-way through the 2004 season, Aston Martin announced a new option for the V12 Vanquish that was called the Sports Dynamic Pack. As its name suggested, it was a group of changes to the suspension, steering and brakes that gave what CEO Dr Ulrich Bez called 'a slightly sportier, more focused approach to the current car'. Bez hoped that it would appeal to a very high proportion of customers, and pointed out that it had been priced to encourage maximum take-up.

The Sports Dynamic Pack, or SDP for short, was first seen in public at the Geneva Motor Show in early March 2004 and became available immediately afterwards. Among other things, it added sales appeal to the V12 Vanquish at a time when rumours of a forthcoming major update might

THERE NEVER WAS A V12 VANQUISH VOLANTE, BUT....

Aston Martin had no plans to build a convertible derivative of the V12 Vanquish, and decided that the DB9 Volante introduced for the 2005 season would cater adequately for customers who wanted an open car. However, the absence of a convertible offering in the first few years of the 2000s left a gap in the market, and unsurprisingly a specialist aftermarket converter found a customer who wanted a convertible Aston Martin just as soon as they could make one.

That company was Newport Convertible Engineering, which was based at Huntington Beach in California. As its name suggests, NCE always specialised in creating convertibles out of closed cars, and its location made it ideally placed to appeal to wealthy celebrities who had chosen to live in California and who were likely to want such cars.

The best information available suggests that just one convertible V12 Vanquish was built, in 2004.

have persuaded some customers to wait for the revised car. That revised car materialised less than six months later as the V12 Vanquish S, and in fact incorporated the revisions of the SDP as standard. According to Aston Martin, just 94 2004-model cars were built with the SDP in the few months when it was available as an option.

The SDP brought thicker and stronger front suspension uprights with shorter springs that lowered the ride height by 5mm, plus different dampers to suit. The steering ratio was raised to make it 20 per cent quicker than before, and there were changes to the brakes. At the front, six-piston callipers and 378mm discs replaced the original four-piston callipers with 355mm discs, while the rear discs were made 2mm thicker than the standard type while retaining their existing 330mm diameter. All the new discs were grooved rather than drilled like the ones they superseded, and the difference could be clearly seen through the new wheels that came as part of the SDP. These wheels had nine slim spokes and a lightweight design that made them 30 per cent less heavy than the standard twelve-spoke type.

THE MID-LIFE 'SPECIALS'

Aston Martin clearly felt that three years on sale was enough without a major change to their flagship model – not least because it had been joined in the showrooms at the start of 2004 by the hugely attractive (though less expensive) DB9 model. They achieved what they wanted in two stages, the first being defined by the appearance of two 'show specials' in early 2004, and the second by a series of upgrades to the production Vanquish that resulted in the Vanquish S some six months later.

The two 'specials' were both displayed at the Geneva International Motor Show in March 2004, just six months after the DB9 had been announced at the 2003 Frankfurt Motor Show. They were well timed: the first examples of the new DB9 had begun to reach customers, and the arrival of the two Vanquish-based show cars not only helped to re-focus attention on the flagship model but also gave the impression that there was a lot going on at Aston Martin. And indeed there was – especially by comparison with the doldrums of the 1970s and 1980s.

Both the show cars had been bodied by Italian coachbuilders, which was a deliberate reminder of Aston Martin's Italian associations in the 1960s, and each had its own interesting story.

According to information released to the media, the Aston Martin Vanquish Zagato Roadster actually grew out of a proposal by the Milanese coachbuilder. The design was drawn up by Nori Harada, Zagato's chief automotive designer, in close co-operation with Peter Hutchinson, the Design Manager at Aston Martin itself. Not surprisingly, it incorporated some very special show-car features, the most interesting of which was a unique design of modular hard- and soft-tops.

The car was designed as a two-seat roadster with a removable hardtop that was carefully created to look as if it was an integral part of the bodywork. When this was removed, the area behind the seats was covered by a hardened glass cover with fairings behind the headrests that recalled the famous Zagato 'double bubble' roofs of the 1960s. The luggage compartment remained visible below the glass, and a simple soft-top stowed in the luggage area could be quickly deployed when necessary.

The Zagato Roadster was a fully drivable car that is generally believed to have been built from a well-used pre-production Vanquish test car. Its registration number (Y823 MWL) was certainly issued in May 2001 by the Oxford licensing authority that covered the Bloxham factory, and was in the same sequence as other known cars that were used for early publicity photography. Its VIN (SCFAC13391B50PP19) also suggests that it started life as the nineteenth pre-production Vanquish. After its Geneva debut, it spent some time on

Aston Martin had no plans for an open Vanquish, and was happy to let Zagato create this roadster from an early pre-production car.

Still very recognisably an Aston Martin, the Zagato roadster had a version of the coachbuilder's trademark 'double-bubble' roof incorporated in the cover panel behind the seats.

The Zagato roadster was a stunning creation from any angle. This one was perhaps most likely to be seen from a hotel balcony!

Zagato nevertheless preferred the centre stack to be coloured to match the rest of the facia, blending it successfully into the overall interior.

The interior layout of the Vanquish remained intact for the Zagato Roadster.

the show circuit, and appeared as an exhibit at the Villa d'Este Concours d'Élégance in Italy and at the Pebble Beach Concours d'Élégance in the USA. An American collector acquired it from the Pebble Beach event, later offering it for sale at the Gooding & Co auction in Arizona where it remained unsold with a high bid of $420,000. It was later offered for sale at a Bonhams auction at the Quail Lodge and Golf Club in Carmel in August 2015, when it sold for $660,000.

It is interesting to compare Zagato's take on the design of the door trims with the standard version, pictured earlier.

The second Vanquish-based 'show special' at Geneva in 2004 was built by Bertone and was known as the Jet 2, a name that followed logically from that of Bertone's 1960 Aston Martin DB4GT Jet. As with the Zagato Roadster, the Bertone Jet 2 was based on a redundant Vanquish test car, but in this case the chassis structure was lengthened by 210mm (8.26in). The vehicle was designed as a two-door shooting brake with seats for four people, and could theoretically have been put into production. In practice, the car returned to Bertone after the Geneva show.

It then re-emerged without warning nine years later at the 2013 Geneva Show, updated with some elements of the second-generation Vanquish and reworked with an opening tailgate, and gold instead of the original silver paint. Its interior had also been retrimmed. By this time the car had become the personal transport of Ermelinda 'Lilli' Bertone, the widow of company founder Nuccio Bertone.

Alongside it on the show stand was a second Bertone Aston Martin, this time based on the company's Rapide model and called the Jet 2+2. This car also had an interesting history. Briton Barry Weir had enquired some time earlier

Bertone's own picture of the Jet 2 car incorporated the obligatory female model. This is it in its original silver finish.

The Bertone design made the car look longer and sleeker than the factory-built Vanquish coupé. Again, this is it in original condition.

The Bertone Jet 2 car was later reworked to incorporate a hatchback, and is shown here in that later guise. Note how the lights were incorporated into a full-width styling feature.

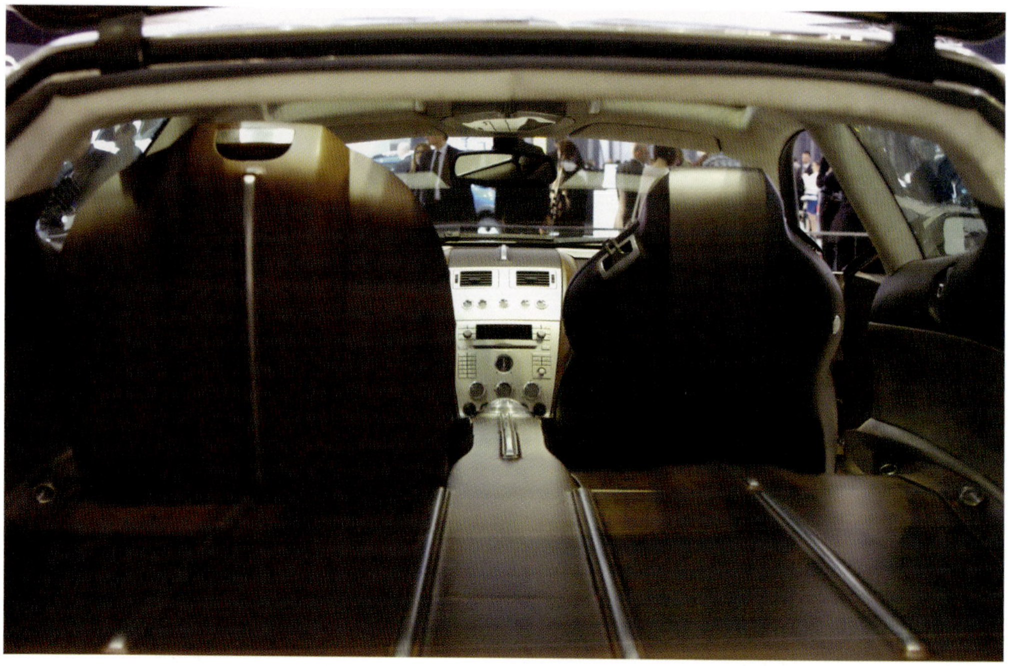

As displayed at the Geneva Show in 2013, Bertone's Jet 2 had easy access to the luggage area behind the two seats.

The later gold finish gave Jet 2 a less clinical appearance than the original silver paint.

whether the original Jet 2 car might be for sale, but Bertone had said no. However, in October 2012 the coachbuilder asked him if he had any interest in a second Jet 2 project. The answer was affirmative; Bertone drew up the plans and Aston Martin agreed that they could go ahead, providing a four-door Rapide saloon as the host vehicle. This arrived in Turin in December 2012, and by the time the Geneva Show opened in March it had been built up as a new car called the Bertone Jet 2+2. Then at the Aston Martin Centenary celebration held at Kensington Palace in London during July 2013, the Jet 2+2, the Jet 2 and the original 1961 Bertone Jet were displayed together.

TECHNICAL SPECIFICATIONS: ASTON MARTIN V12 VANQUISH

Engine
All-alloy V12 with 4 valves per cylinder.
5935cc (89mm bore x 79.5 stroke).
Four chain-driven overhead camshafts.
10.5:1 CR.
Visteon Twin PTEC engine management system and sequential fuel injection:
460bhp at 6,500rpm
400lb ft at 5,000rpm

Gearbox
Six-speed manual with clutchless electronic paddle-shift gear selection and full automatic control mode.

Final drive
3.69:1, with limited-slip differential.

Suspension
Front suspension with double wishbones, coil springs, gas dampers and anti-roll bar.
Rear suspension with double wishbones, coil springs, gas dampers and anti-roll bar.

Steering
Rack-and-pinion system with variable power assistance.
20 per cent quicker ratio on cars fitted with Sports Dynamic Pack.

Brakes
Brembo four-piston callipers front and rear, acting on ventilated and cross-drilled discs with a 355mm (14in) diameter at the front and a 330mm (13in) diameter at the rear.
Cars with the Sports Dynamic Pack have Brembo six-piston front and four-piston rear callipers, acting on ventilated and cross-drilled discs with a 378mm (14.9in) diameter at the front and a 330mm (13in) diameter at the rear.
Teves ABS system; with EBD from the 2004 model-year.

Wheels and tyres
19in (483mm) cast magnesium wheels, 9J x 19 at the front and 10J x 19 at the rear.
Yokohama AV S Sport tyres, 255/40ZR19 at the front and 285/40ZR19 at the rear.

Dimensions

Overall length:	4,665mm (183.66in)
Overall width:	1,923mm (75.7in); 1,998mm (78.6in) over mirrors
Overall height:	1,318mm (51.9in)
Wheelbase:	2,690mm (105.9in)
Track, front:	1,572mm (61.9in)
Track, rear:	1,584mm (62.3in)

Weight
1,835kg (4,045lb) kerb weight

CHAPTER 4

THE V12 VANQUISH S, 2004–2007

The rumours turned out to be true: Aston Martin announced the new 2005-model V12 Vanquish S at the Paris Motor Show in 2004, early in the traditional European motor show season. Priced rather higher than the last of the original V12 Vanquish cars, at £174,000, the new model incorporated a number of exterior and interior cosmetic changes, as well as the suspension, steering and brake changes that had been previewed a few months earlier in the Sports Dynamic Pack. However, the headline news was that this latest version of the Aston Martin flagship really was capable of exceeding the 320km/h (200mph) that had been suggested for the Project Vantage concept car back in 1998.

Two major changes had brought the 320km/h (200mph) within reach. First was continuous development of the V12 engine, which in Vanquish S guise now delivered 520bhp at its 6,500rpm power peak, together with 435lb ft (576Nm) of torque at 5,000rpm. These higher figures had been achieved through improvements to the airflow via fully machined inlet ports and combustion chambers, matched to new injectors, forged conrods, different sparkplugs and a remapped engine

Finished in one of the metallic greys that were so popular on these cars, this is a 2007-model V12 Vanquish S.

Looking every inch the expensive GT, this black Vanquish S is an early one, without the radio aerial at the back of the roof.

Superficially similar to the twelve-spoke wheels on the earlier cars, those on the Vanquish S had just eleven spokes.

ECU. The second change was to a taller 4.3:1 final drive, which was just enough to get the car over that 320km/h (200mph) target – although it was also just enough to take the edge off acceleration, and the 0–60mph time quoted for the Vanquish S was usually 4.8sec, or around 0.2sec longer than the earlier 460bhp car. (Even so, road tests found that it actually accelerated better than the old car.)

New Vanquish S tail badging made it easy to identify one of the revised models, although this could be deleted on customer request, so it was fortunate that there were other features to aid recognition. The front end was endowed with a larger grille distinguished by six horizontal bars that was intended to improve engine cooling, and there was a discreet front 'splitter' below the existing spoiler. In tandem with a new spoiler integrated into the boot lid (and embracing a high-level third brake light, moved from its earlier position behind the rear window), this reduced the drag coefficient to 0.32 from the 0.33 of the earlier Vanquish. The tail spoiler was also claimed to reduce rear-end lift at high speeds and so to improve stability. Meanwhile a new wheel design was only to be expected, and Aston Martin obliged with an attractive eleven-spoke type, forged rather than cast like its predecessors and so shaving a total of 33lb off the unsprung weight to the benefit of both handling and ride.

Not every 2005-model V12 Vanquish was a Vanquish S, because the last of the original models were sold alongside the new one. (For the record, the first production Vanquish S was numbered 1506.) By the time the last order for the original model had been completed, Aston Martin had built 1,503 examples of the car. For the 2006 season, the Vanquish S would then become the only derivative on sale

This head-on view of a late Vanquish S shows the extra splitter below the front bumper and the new grille in its enlarged opening.

THE COST WHEN NEW: ASTON MARTIN V12 VANQUISH S

The following are base prices, without special options and extras.

	UK	USA
Vanquish S, 2004	£174,000	
Vanquish S, 2005		$255,000
Vanquish S, 2007	£182,095	
Vanquish 25, 2021	£550,000	

WHAT THE PRESS THOUGHT OF THE VANQUISH S

When British magazine *Autocar* reported on its test of a Vanquish S in the issue dated 17 May 2005, it could hardly have been more complimentary. The testers said that the car 'makes a compelling case for itself beside any rival, at any price' and 'distances itself sufficiently from the DB9 to make sense as a stand-alone model at the top of Aston Martin's increasingly impressive range of cars. Warts and all, we think it's fabulous.' For good measure, they went on to add that this was 'the fastest and best Vanquish – and Aston – ever.'

There was only really one 'wart' that the magazine highlighted, and this was that the car suffered from brake fade after repeated stops. As for performance, 'the S isn't just slightly quicker [than the earlier Vanquish]: it's much quicker.' It took nearly 2sec less to accelerate from 80km/h (50mph) to 112km/h (70mph) in top gear, and the 0–100mph dash was achieved in 10sec dead as against 10.4sec for the earlier car. That was on a surface that was less than ideally grippy; the magazine estimated that a 9.5sec time would have been achieved on a better surface.

The news for everyday driving was good, too, because 'the way you access the performance is now so much clearer

The Vanquish S had a revised boot lid, this time incorporating the high-level third brake light within an aerodynamic spoiler. The rear bumper apron incorporates the sensors for a radar parking distance system.

Mesh grilles for the bonnet vents....

... and for the vents in the front wings as well.

Exquisite detail: the fuel filler cap in the left-hand rear wing.

Just in case onlookers needed any confirmation, there was a Vanquish S badge on the car's tail....

... and there was further conformation etched into the sill plates.

thanks to a much-improved paddle-shift gearbox.' And although this was 'not a cutting-edge sports car', it was a 'comfortable GT that will, if pushed, corner hard enough and crisply enough for 99 per cent of drivers... even in extremis, it's a delightfully benign handler.'

Over in the USA, *Sports Car International* published a test (by the British writer Ian Kuah) in its May 2005 issue. A special concern was how the car matched up to its Ferrari 575M Maranello rival, because it had obviously been intended to take on the Italian car as well as 'to put clear air between the flagship Aston and the DB9' by offering demonstrably more for its higher price.

Overall, the Vanquish S was 'a genuine step forward in all the areas that count: acceleration, turn-in, handling grip and braking are all a notch better. Yet... the ride has not suffered unduly.' The brakes were 'immensely powerful and fade-free, and thanks to a redesigned pedal box with better operating geometry, pedal feel and travel are improved as well.' On the down side, its Yokohama tyres were noisier than the Bridgestones now fitted to the DB9 – but there was particular praise for the car's 'bombastic' acceleration: 'dip into the throttle at just about any speed and the big V12 deepens its baritone voice and delivers instant and relentless thrust.' And, importantly, it sounded good, too: 'the soundtrack of this car resoundingly beats that of its rival from Italy ... the Ferrari is far too quiet... [and] sounds rather ordinary.'

THE FINAL YEARS

Modern supercars tend to have a relatively short shelf life, and the arrival of the Vanquish S had been timed for just past the intended mid-life of the Vanquish models. Customers at that end of the market are often interested mainly in having the latest sensation (which is a quite different viewpoint from that of the ordinary enthusiast), and a car that has been on the market for five years is already beginning to look like yesterday's news. Anxious that the Vanquish S should not suffer as a result, Aston Martin decided to give it a further makeover for the 2006 season.

This time, the focus was on the passenger cabin, where the newer DB9 models had been making the pace. The 2006 Vanquish S came with a redesigned dashboard centre stack that drew on DB9 practice, and was trimmed in leather instead of being painted. In cars for most countries it had a new 16cm (6.5in) satellite navigation screen that has since attracted the nickname of 'big screen cars' for the

The V12 nestled in its usual place under the bonnet, but now had an S on the cover plate between its cylinder banks.

The passenger cabin was carefully trimmed to provide a luxury GT ambience. This one is in a later example of the Vanquish S.

The centre stack was revised on the later cars, and for most markets incorporated a satellite navigation screen. Other switchgear was rearranged to make room.

late model Vanquish S types. This screen was essentially the same Volvo-sourced item that was also used in the DB9, and was not universally liked. The satellite navigation system was of course not fitted on cars delivered to countries where there was no mapping data for it.

The new satellite navigation screen required a reorganisation of some of the switchgear, and the starter button and gear selector switches were moved further down. So was the clock, which ended up so much further down that it must have become almost invisible to some drivers. Further changes brought climate control knobs similar to those in the DB9, together with a Bluetooth phone-pairing system, and a change to the cupholder so beloved of US buyers. More important, perhaps, was a new Aston Martin-branded 900-watt Alpine ICE system that now replaced the earlier Linn system. This was accompanied on the outside of the car by a rakishly angled radio aerial mounted to the rear of the roof.

The 2006 season would be the last one when the Vanquish S was available in the USA, and the last US example was delivered in June 2006. This early end to sales was brought about by a change in US Federal legal requirements, which for 2007 demanded automatic deactivation of the passenger's side airbag when a child (under a certain weight) was using the associated seat. As the Vanquish S was already scheduled to be replaced in 2007, Aston Martin decided that sales were unlikely to justify the re-engineering that would be needed to incorporate the new feature, and withdrew the car from sale instead.

Modern digital readouts and lights mingle with traditional analogue instruments on the dashboard of a Vanquish S, and of course the rev counter carries a winged Aston Martin logo.

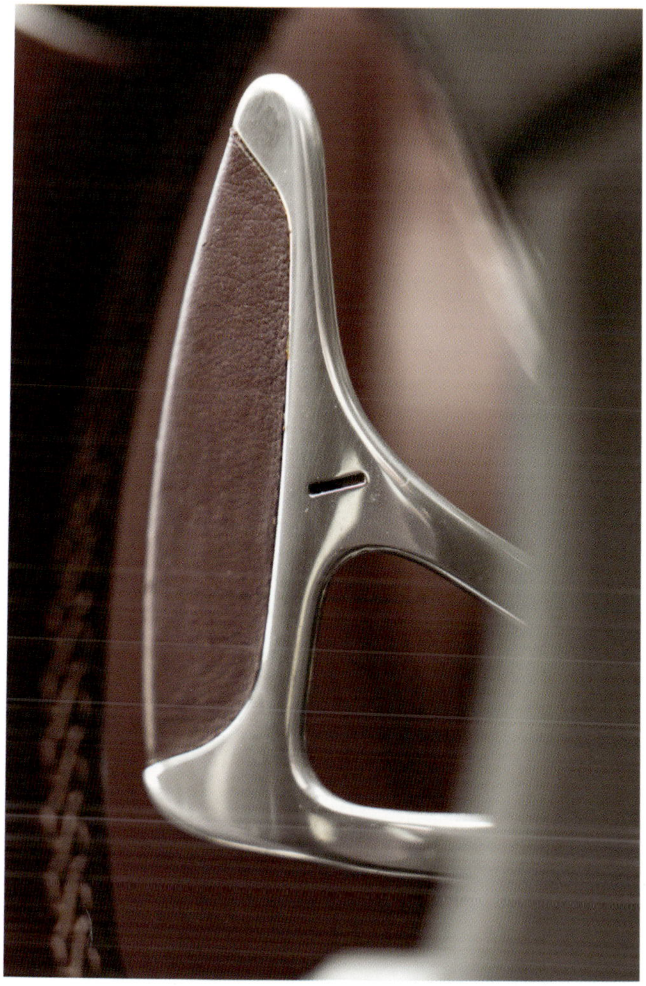

The paddle-switch gearbox was unchanged in its essentials from the one on the earlier cars, but the paddles themselves were now trimmed to match the interior.

Later seats had 'wings' for extra support.

The end of production in summer 2007 was marked with a special edition that was (somewhat unimaginatively) named as the Vanquish S Ultimate Edition. Announced in February 2007, this was originally intended to consist of 40 cars, but every single one of the 40 was sold within a few weeks of the announcement. As a result, Aston Martin extended the total to 50, and in the end there were twenty cars with right-hand drive and 30 with left-hand drive.

The Ultimate Edition is generally regarded as encompassing the last 50 cars to be built, but in practice that was not quite the case. Tim Cottingham (of astonmartins.com) reports that there were four white cars among the last ones built, of which three were a special edition for the UAE, and that there was at least one other special order. (For more detail on these cars, see panel.)

The Ultimate Edition cars were painted in a new metallic Ultimate Black colour that remained unique to these last models of the V12 Vanquish. Otherwise, from the outside these looked like standard cars, and only a discreet badge on the wing vent confirmed what they were. There were more differences inside, however, which began with personalised sill plates that carried the car's limited-edition number. All the cars were two-seaters, with a cabin trimmed in semi-aniline leather (where the pigmentation does not conceal the natural grain or the hair pores) that featured fashionable coarse stitching. Some of the interior fittings had a black chrome finish, and there was a leather headlining. By this

SOME OTHER LATE 'SPECIALS'

Among the final examples of the V12 Vanquish S to be built at Newport Pagnell were at least four cars painted Morning Frost white. Three of them were built for customers in the United Arab Emirates, and these had specially engraved sill plates showing that they belonged to a limited run of three.

Aston Martin was also experimenting with transparent roofs at the time, and the four-door Rapide concept displayed at the Detroit motor show in January 2006 had one, made of lightweight polycarbonate. It appears that a number of similar roofs (though without the ability to turn opaque) were made to suit the Vanquish S, and at least three cars were fitted with them.

Among those three, the best known is the 'Copper Kettle', which was given a special name as part of a tradition that originated with Lionel Martin's wife. This was built to special order for a customer in the spring and summer of 2007 with the participation of Aston Martin Works Service, and incorporated several other special features. It was first seen in public at the Aston Martin Owners' Club's Autumn Concours at Chatsworth House in September 2007, and was also described in an issue of the *AM Magazine* produced for customers.

The car was painted in a specially developed colour called Copper Chestnut, and its transparent roof had a heat-reflective coating to help maintain acceptable interior temperatures. The front end featured concealed parking sensors and horizontal bright grille bars, while the wings carried 'Works Prepared' badges and the fuel filler cap was etched with the logo of HWM, the supplying dealer in Walton-on-Thames. The passenger cabin was trimmed in Saddle Tan leather with Tan Alcantara panels and contrasting Sandstorm carpet. Door-handle escutcheons and the interior light housings were painted to match the exterior, and there was perforated leather on the steering-wheel rim.

All-Black: this realistic-looking rendering of the Ultimate Edition was produced in 2007 within Aston Martin.

The last production Vanquish was a Vanquish S Ultimate Edition. The Newport Pagnell workforce gather to wish it farewell.

The Ultimate Edition cars all had a numbered sill plate like this.

THE BONIOLO V12 VANQUISH EG SHOOTING BRAKE, 2007

The year 2007 also saw the appearance of a one-off shooting brake conversion based on the V12 Vanquish. Commissioned by an anonymous customer, who nevertheless lent his initials of EG to the car's name, it was designed by Francesco Boniolo in Italy and constructed by Quality Cars of Vigonza.

The specially commissioned Boniolo EG Shooting Brake was a sleek and elegant one-off.

The Shooting Brake was built on a lengthened Vanquish platform to give room for four passengers, and rear doors were engineered into the design to improve access.

Boniolo established a design and architecture studio in 1975, and worked in several sectors, including that of automotive design. In this case, his design called for a lengthened chassis to make room for proper rear seats, which were flanked by additional rearward-opening doors. Like the Aston Martin Rapide concept, the shooting brake had a full-length transparent roof of Isolite glass that could be made opaque by pressing a button on the dashboard. Boniolo claimed that the Hawker Hurricane and Supermarine Spitfire, both British World War II fighter aircraft, had an influence on the car's shape.

The car was painted in traditional British Racing Green, and the cabin was trimmed in lobster-coloured leather by Pineider, with bamboo wood finishers on the doors and dashboard.

The Shooting Brake was a remarkably good-looking car from all angles, and still retained some of the Vanquish styling elements.

The lobster-red interior contrasted sharply but superbly with the British Racing Green exterior. Note the contrasting lighter covering for the centre stack.

There was just enough room in the rear for small children, but this was really a 2+2 rather than a full four-seater. The sill plate has the EG initials of the owner.

time, the cost of a V12 Vanquish S had risen to £182,095 in the UK, but there was no additional cost for the Ultimate Edition cars, which were simply available on request by a customer.

The very last car that came off the lines in July 2007 had chassis number 502589, and was initially retained by Aston Martin for promotional purposes, although has since been sold into private hands. It most certainly was a significant car, because it was not only the last V12 Vanquish S, but also the very last Aston Martin to be built at Newport Pagnell before the factory was turned over to other purposes. In future, the company planned to go for higher production volumes than were possible with the essentially traditional construction methods used at the factory that had been its home since 1955.

A total of 1,086 Vanquish S models had come from the Newport Pagnell works. Added to the 1,503 'standard' V12 Vanquish types built between 2001 and 2004, that made a grand total of 2,589 Vanquish models – a figure confirmed by the 502589 serial number of the last car. The Vanquish name then lapsed for a while, as the new DBS model became the Aston Martin flagship in 2007 – but the Vanquish name was too good to be forgotten, and it was revived just five years later for the car that replaced the DBS in 2012.

AN AFTERLIFE

Production of the original Vanquish may have ended in 2007, but the cars are very much still alive thanks to aftermarket specialists and to Aston Martin Works and the Vanquish's original designer, Ian Callum.

Aston Martin Works

Not everybody liked the paddle-shift gearbox that was the only option available for the Vanquish and Vanquish S models, and about a year before production ended a retro-fit alternative was made available by Aston Martin Works, the heritage arm of the company. This replaced the original gearbox by a conventional six-speed manual type, and of course added a conventional clutch as well. Customers' cars could be converted either at Aston Martin Works itself or by authorised dealers outside the UK. In the UK, the conversion was initially priced at £13,250 (plus VAT at the prevailing rate, of course), and in the first few years around a dozen cars a year were submitted for conversion.

This was a very neat conversion, and more or less undetectable to anyone not familiar with the cars. It used the gear lever from the V8 Vantage model, which occupied the position that on early cars belonged to the cupholder. On the 2006 and later models, where the cupholder was in a different place, it took the position of the ash tray, and part of the centre stack had to be recessed to allow enough room for the gear lever to reach its forward positions. On cars of all ages, the paddle-shifts were of course removed as well, and their mounting holes were concealed by re-covering the steering-wheel cowl.

An additional service available from Aston Martin Works was replacement of the original aluminium-finish garnish panels in the passenger cabin. Seen as edgy and avant-garde when new, they soon became rather less so, and Vanquish owners began to call for alternatives. As a result, Aston Martin Works began to offer the options of genuine carbon-fibre panels and a choice of three different walnut wood finishes.

Kahn Design

Kahn Design was (and still is) a British company based in Bradford that specialised in high-end bespoke automotive conversions. These ranged from major work that included full retrims and bodykits, to replacement wheels and smaller accessories. The work of Afzal Kahn's company sometimes carried the Project Kahn brand, and there were several options available for the Aston Martin Vanquish. Among these were several designs of the 20in wheel, and twin stainless-steel strakes in place of the single standard one over each front wing air vent.

Vanquish 25 by Callum

At the time he designed the 1998 Project Vanquish concept car, Ian Callum was Chief Designer of the TWR Design consultancy, and before the car reached production as the Vanquish in 2001 he had moved on to become Design Director for Jaguar. Eighteen years later he stepped down from that position, and very quickly established Ian Callum Design as a consultancy business. A year after that, he announced the Vanquish 25, a restoration and update package for the car he had designed that was intended to 'make the Vanquish the Grand Tourer for the 2020s'.

'It's rare that a designer has the chance to retell the story of one of their own cars,' Callum explained when the car was launched. 'I've wanted to do that for some time. Materials and technologies have advanced, allowing us to introduce these along with new ideas that weren't feasible when the car was launched.'

The project was co-funded by R-Reforged, a Swiss-based company that had its own race team, made a speciality out of low-volume specials, and also had links with the Swiss Aston Martin importer. The cars, meanwhile, were produced at Callum Design's own premises in Warwickshire. Their numbers were to be strictly limited to 25 examples – hence the Vanquish 25 name – and these comprehensively uprated and restyled cars were to be built on a bespoke basis, incorporating a claimed 350 or more changes from the original production specification. As for cost, around £550,000 was the starting price, including purchase of a suitable Vanquish for conversion.

From the start, the aim was not only to increase the performance, but also to make the Vanquish more of a driver's car, to eliminate the niggles and dynamic weaknesses that had marred the original, and to make the car a competitive purchase in its class more than twenty years after the first examples left the production lines at Newport Pagnell. Lead engineer on the project was Adam Donfrancesco, who had earlier worked at Aston Martin on the development of cars such as the GT8 and GT12 limited-production race-inspired derivatives of the Vantage, but who had also spent time with Noble Automotive and Jaguar Land Rover.

An obvious requirement was to increase the engine power, and this was achieved mainly through work on the cylinder heads and careful calibration, along with a new exhaust system. Here, the manifolds were pulse-tuned to reduce back pressure, and the rest of the system was redesigned with a shaped underside to the silencer that doubled as the upper surface of the rear diffuser. This change not only removed any need for an additional under tray, but also improved the dissipation of heat. And, needless to say, the main silencer box had also been acoustically tuned to deliver more exciting noises – a 'cultured yowl' as *Top Gear* writer Jason Barlow put it. The revised engine laid claim to 580bhp, an increase of 60bhp over the last Vanquish S of thirteen years earlier, and was more willing to rev than Aston Martin's own version. Torque was up by 51lb ft, and for good measure, the Vanquish 25 had also undergone some cosmetic work in the engine bay: the V12 was set off with a new carbon-fibre induction manifold and new cam covers.

Customers could order a Vanquish 25 with its original paddle-shift gearbox, although that had never been much liked because of its jerky changes, which could sometimes feel slow, too. So it was offered with the options of the six-speed manual conversion that was already available from Aston Martin Works, or a six-speed automatic manufactured by GM. The car that *Evo* magazine drove in 2022 had the six-speed manual, which 'has a transformative effect on the Vanquish driving experience by immediately immersing you in the process of driving.'

Extensive chassis development had made the car feel tauter than the original, but it still worked well as a grand tourer. *Evo* thought that it felt less bulky, too. The wheels retained the original 'factory' spoked design but were now a size larger, with a 20in diameter and cutting-edge Michelin Pilot Sport S tyres to improve grip. Stiffer anti-roll bars, new suspension bushes and retuned Bilstein dampers all made their own contribution to the transformation, as did a 10mm (0.4in) reduction in the ride height, and track increases of 50mm (2in) at the front and 33mm (1.3in) at the rear. As for the brakes, the original ventilated discs had given way to an adaptation of Aston Martin's later carbon-ceramic system, with 398mm front discs and 360mm discs at the rear, which gave a firmer pedal along with more than adequate stopping power.

'It's categorically not the sort of machine you fling down an undulating, unpredictable B-road with impunity,' reported *Top Gear* magazine after driving an early example in 2020, 'but it is easier and much more satisfying to drive quickly, and turns in with a much greater sense of commitment [than the original Vanquish].'

A good deal of work had also gone into the interior, and the driving position had been improved by redesigned seats that allowed their occupants to sit lower in the car, whilst a spacer adjusted the position of the steering wheel for a perfect match. Even the steering wheel had been modified to give a better feel, its rim milled to reduce the overall diameter and then retrimmed. 'Where it always felt like you were perched on top of the Vanquish,' said *Top Gear* magazine in 2020, 'now you're properly *in* it.' All the Vanquish 25 cars were planned as two-seaters, and the token '+2' rear seats had been very sensibly abandoned in favour of a luggage platform adorned with bespoke luggage made by Mulberry.

In place of the much-criticised dashboard centre stack with its silver paint, the Vanquish 25 had a redesigned carbon-fibre section with a big wraparound metal frame. Modern tastes had been accommodated with an up-to-date ICE system and Apple Car Play, while the instruments and a detachable pocket watch in its own cradle on top of the centre console were all beautifully crafted by the British luxury watchmaker Bremont. Leather specialist Bridge of

Weir had also provided a new signature tartan for the seats, reflecting Ian Callum's Scottish ancestry.

Last but by no means least, there were the exterior changes that Callum had wrought. The larger-diameter wheels made a further contribution here, and the wider tracks helped them to fill the wheel-arches. The reprofiled front bumper was now made of carbon fibre and incorporated brake cooling ducts, while the grille was now machined from billet, and the bonnet vents had what Callum called an 'abstract tartan' mesh. New sills, carbon-fibre side strakes, bespoke door mirrors, one-piece carbon-fibre window surrounds and a fuel filler that combined aluminium and carbon fibre all added more modern touches to a design that had in any case worn very well.

'What you appreciate very quickly,' reported *Evo* magazine, 'is that this isn't a half-hearted revamp. The new headlamp and tail-light units, for example, are ferociously expensive – circa £500k – to have manufactured (and Type Approved) in such small volumes. It's items such as this that are indicative of the lengths Callum and R-Reforged have gone to.'

TECHNICAL SPECIFICATIONS: ASTON MARTIN V12 VANQUISH S

Engine
All-alloy V12 with 4 valves per cylinder.
5935cc (89mm bore x 79.5 stroke).
Four chain-driven overhead camshafts.
Compression ratio 10.8:1.
Visteon Twin PTEC engine management system and sequential fuel injection:
520bhp at 6,500rpm
435lb ft at 5,000rpm

Gearbox
Six-speed manual with clutchless electronic paddle-shift gear selection and full automatic control mode.

Final drive
4.30:1

Suspension
Front suspension with double wishbones, coil springs, gas dampers and anti-roll bar.
Rear suspension with double wishbones, coil springs, gas dampers and anti-roll bar.

Steering
Rack-and-pinion system with variable power assistance.

Brakes
Brembo six-piston front and four-piston rear callipers, acting on ventilated and cross-drilled discs with a 378mm (14.9in) diameter at the front and a 330mm (13in) diameter at the rear.
Teves ABS system with EBD.

Wheels and tyres
19in (483mm) cast magnesium wheels, 9J x 19 at the front and 10J x 19 at the rear.
Yokohama AV S Sport tyres, 255/40ZR19 at the front and 285/40ZR19 at the rear.

Dimensions

Overall length:	4,665mm (183.66in)
Overall width:	1,998mm (78.6in) over mirrors
Overall height:	1,318mm (51.9in)
Wheelbase:	2,690mm (105.9in)
Track, front:	1,572mm (61.9in)
Track, rear:	1,584mm (62.3in)

Weight
1,875kg (4,134lb)

CHAPTER 5

A NEW DB MODEL

When Ford appointed Dr Ulrich Bez as the new CEO and Chairman of Aston Martin in July 2000, the forward model plan was one that had been drawn up in the later 1990s. At the top of the range, the V12 Vanquish was intended to be the first of the new high-tech Astons for the twenty-first century, and it was already nearly ready for its introduction in 2001. The 'junior' model DB7, if it can be called that without giving offence to its legions of enthusiastic owners, was going to be replaced in due course by a car that had the project code name of AM802, and this was conceived as a 2+2 GT model.

There was also a third project in the wings, a smaller two-seater car that was intended to compete with other high-performance cars such as the Porsche 911 and the Ferrari 360. This project had the code name of AM305, and was conceived as a mid-engined car. That would have made it very different from the traditional front-engined, rear-wheel-drive Aston Martin, but it was not the company's first look at such a layout. The legendary 1979 Bulldog concept car had also been mid-engined, although as explained in Chapter 1, it never reached production.

Ulrich Bez had a distinguished automotive background. In the 1980s he had led R&D and motor-sport programmes at Porsche, and had subsequently joined BMW as the first director of its advanced technology division, BMW Technik. There he had overseen the development and launch of the

The AM305 project for a smaller, mid-engined car was shelved in 2001.

This rear view of an AM305 mock-up shows that by this time Aston Martin was wedded to sleek, aerodynamic shapes.

revolutionary ZI sports car. A stint as engineering chief with Daewoo in the 1990s was followed by a period as a consultant for Ford, until that company decided that its British PAG brands needed to be separately managed.

Quite clearly, Bez was expected to improve the performance of the Aston Martin business, and equally clearly he had been told that he could draw on Ford's immense global resources to help him to do so. He lost no time in making some changes. One of the first was to terminate the project for the mid-engined car, AM305, which he apparently did on his second day with the company. That reduced the risk of spreading the company's resources too thinly: a two-model range was all it needed, in his opinion. He also lost no time in reviewing the V12 Vanquish and, as Chapter 2 explains, decided to delay its introduction in order to give his teams time to improve the interior of the passenger cabin.

Bez also looked at the 2+2 GT project, AM802, and decided that that was not the best way forwards. The company had already spent large sums of Ford money on developing the advanced new bonded composite structure for the Vanquish, and it would simply be wasteful to make that exclusive to the flagship model and to develop another new structure for the DB7 replacement. It would be a much more sensible use of time and resources to develop the new structure further, and to ensure that it was flexible enough to underpin multiple new models in the future. They would include a new project for the DB7's replacement.

THE VH PLATFORM

So it was that Bez initiated the design and development of such a flexible structure. Most of the work was done during 2001, and of course Aston Martin drew on the resources of the Ford Motor Company, as well as their own. The essence of the Lotus-developed structure was retained, but changes were made so that it could be relatively easily adapted to suit cars of different sizes. Some changes were made to improve efficiency during assembly, with the result that the revised body assembly would take only 30 minutes to complete, as against four hours for the earlier Vanquish structure. This represented a considerable and very welcome cost saving.

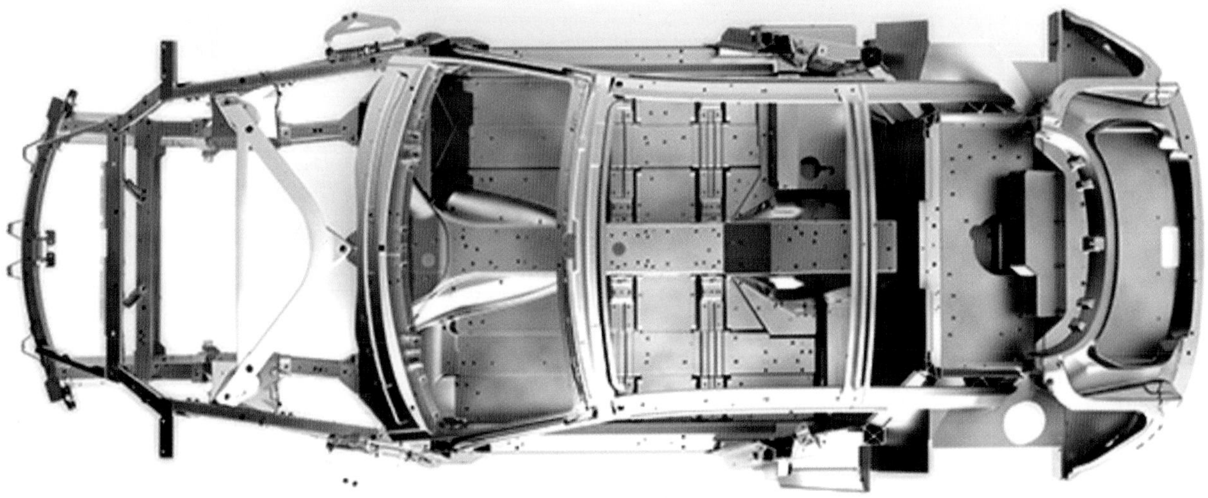

The VH structure was a further development of the bodyshell designed earlier for the 2001 Vanquish.

ASTON MARTIN AND THE VH PLATFORM

Although the structure designed by Aston Martin in conjunction with Lotus for the 2001 Vanquish model pioneered some of the aluminium bonding techniques that characterised the VH platform, it was not itself a VH platform. 'We learned a lot about aluminium structures from Vanquish,' DB9 Chief Programme Engineer Dave King told *European Automotive Design* for its November 2003 issue, 'but with its combination of steel, aluminium and composite it is quite a complex and costly assembly not really suited to the DB9's bigger production run.'

The VH platform used for the DB9 was significantly different from the 'original' structure for the Vanquish. Aston Martin's Chief Body Engineer Andy Syvret told *European Automotive Design*:

> *One major difference lay in the way it had grown into an integrated body frame. Instead of the centre section being a bolted and bonded hybrid assembly, this is a more unitary construction of one technology throughout the car. It is largely extruded, with cast and folded or stamped sheet metal parts in whatever is the most cost-effective, weight-efficient and structural application. The sill and the cantrail sections round the doors are extrusions. The front suspension mounts and body interfaces are machine castings to provide the required geometry and strength. All are now bonded using proven high temperature epoxy adhesive between aluminium.*

The DB9 was the first production Aston Martin to use the VH platform, and this version of the structure was always considered to be the first generation of the design. A second-generation VH structure then appeared in the V8 Vantage model of 2005. This second-generation structure demonstrated the versatility of the VH platform concept when it was used in several models of different sizes: the 2007 Aston Martin DBS, the 2011 Aston Martin Zagato (based on a Vantage S), and the 2014 bespoke Aston Martin DB10 concept car that appeared in the James Bond 007 film *Spectre* released in 2015.

The third generation of the VH platform was used for the 2011 Aston Martin Virage, for the DB9 from 2012 (on the 2013 facelift models), and for later derivatives of the Aston Martin Vanquish. The fourth generation of the platform was an extended and re-engineered version of this that was used for the 2010 Aston Martin Rapide and its variants, and for the 2019 Aston Martin Vanquish Zagato Shooting Brake.

The versatility of the VH platform is well demonstrated by the fact that it has been used for the four-door Rapide as well as for several two-door Aston Martin models. Its weight-saving qualities are illustrated by the fact that a DB9 bodyshell weighed 25 per cent less than the steel bodyshell of its DB7 predecessor and yet had twice the torsional rigidity.

The new structure became known as the 'VH' platform, the two letters simply standing for 'vertical-horizontal'. The 'vertical' part meant that the platform could be used up and down the Aston Martin range: it was engineered to be stretchable or shrinkable to whatever size future new models might require. The 'horizontal' part suggested that elements of it could be shared between different Aston Martin models, such as the suspension components. The VH platform was therefore a dimensionally flexible structure that was intended to serve Aston Martin for a good many years: length, wheelbase and tracks could be changed to suit the requirements of various front-engined formats, and in this way it would save the cost and difficulty of designing a new platform every time a new model was required. In practice it would last for nearly thirteen years, and would underpin every new model between 2003 and 2016. (See the sidebar.)

Developing existing technology rather than having to grapple with something new and different also meant that the DB7 replacement could be ready in a relatively short time. The new car could, of course, use the V12 engine that was already in production – although it would have to have a lower state of tune than in the Vanquish out of respect for the position of that model at the top of the Aston Martin hierarchy.

While the engineers worked on the design and development of the new Aston Martin, the marketing teams were working on what to call it. As a replacement for the DB7, it would most logically retain the DB letters in its name for the sake of continuity. Yet the DB8 name did not sound right, for reasons that are explained in the next chapter. The final solution was to skip the number 8 in the sequence and to call it a DB9.

THE V12 ENGINE

By the time work began on the DB9 at Aston Martin, the V12 engine had become a well-established part of the company repertoire. It had earned its reputation initially in the DB7 Vantage, and would go on to enhance that reputation from 2001 in the Vanquish. Yet even though it was considered to be Aston Martin 'property', Ford still maintained a distant oversight. Cosworth still remained involved too, not only casting the alloy cylinder blocks and cylinder heads for Aston Martin, but actually assembling the complete 5953cc engines as well.

Further development of the engine for the DB9 was nevertheless an Aston Martin responsibility, and was entrusted to the company's chief powertrain engineer, Dr Brian Fitzsimmons. He ran a small team within Aston Martin itself while also overseeing the work of a dozen engineers at the Ford advanced research laboratory in the USA. This joint British and American team made changes to the crankshaft, the camshafts, the manifolds, the lubrication and the management system of the existing production V12 to deliver an engine that offered 450bhp at 6,000rpm.

This state of tune had been chosen to help position the DB9 below the 460bhp Vanquish, while making clear that the new car was more powerful than the 420bhp DB7 that it replaced (and more powerful than the late-model DB7 Vantage GT that had 429bhp). A satisfyingly wide spread of torque had been achieved by careful tuning of the inlet manifold lengths, and of the peak 420lb ft (570Nm) that was generated at 5,000rpm, no less than 85 per cent was available at 1,500rpm. And, of course, the latest DB9 version of the engine not only met all current and anticipated emissions regulations but also incorporated a bypass valve in its exhaust to create a superb soundtrack for the occupants of the car.

When interviewed for the November 2003 issue of *European Automotive Design* magazine, Fitzsimmons was keen to point out that this latest, third-generation version of the V12 engine was a world first in its use of a neural network management system, which used Ford software adapted to meet the Aston Martin requirements. Neural networks replicate as closely as possible the processes of the human brain, and in this case the software was used to simplify the engine knock detection system. Instead of individual misfire detection sensors for each cylinder (as on the earlier Vanquish

The 6.0-litre V12 engine was set well back in the engine bay in the interests of even weight distribution.

V12), the new 'intelligent' system used a single proximity sensor to detect speed fluctuations on the flywheel. The system made measurements every 1.39 seconds, and the engine management system was then able to take corrective action within 16.7 milliseconds when necessary.

'The advantage,' explained Fitzsimmons, 'is that it is non-intrusive, and actually learns the engine's characteristics within a couple of minutes, and will adjust for changes in performance and pick out a misfire however it is caused, through poor quality fuel or whatever.'

As compared to the Vanquish V12, the DB9 engine also had a major change to its exhaust manifolds. The Vanquish engine used six separate catalytic converters, which were not only an expensive solution but also led to high under-bonnet temperatures. For the DB9, the Aston Martin team developed a different system, with two small catalytic converters mounted as closely as possible to each exhaust manifold and serving three cylinders each. These then led to a larger third 'cat', again one for each cylinder bank, which was mounted under the floor of the car to keep heat out of the engine bay.

The engine retained the hollow camshaft design and the lighter crankshaft of the Vanquish type, although these now came from a different supplier, identified only as being involved in Formula One work. These items minimised the weight of the reciprocating masses. Meanwhile, a pair of Visteon engine controllers treated each bank as an individual 6-cylinder engine. There were two safety controllers, and a monitor that co-ordinated all the systems and synchronised the twin electronically controlled throttles.

One other special feature of the DB9 engine – or rather, of its installation – deserves comment here. In order to achieve optimum weight distribution, the engine was mounted quite a long way back in the car, behind the front wheels. Some commentators have even gone so far as to describe the car as being mid-front-engined. The effect of this layout was to set the two rearmost cylinders of the engine below the bulkhead, which inevitably compromised ease of servicing. Aston Martin dealt with this in two ways, on the one hand providing removable access panels, and on the other standardising long-life sparkplugs, which of course were used for all twelve cylinders.

The specification of the Aston Martin V12 did not stand still during the twelve-year production life of the DB9. As the later chapters of this book explain, its peak power went up from the initial 450bhp to 470bhp in 2008, to 510bhp in 2013, and then to 540bhp in 2015. Later versions in other models have become even more powerful.

Aston Martin were never very keen on commentators raking over the story behind their V12 engine, which they saw very much as their own creation. Nevertheless, as late as February 2017, two years after the DB9 had gone out of production, an Aston Martin special supplement in *Classic & Sportscar* magazine was still arguing that, 'in essence, the AM04 is a brace of Ford Duratecc V6s nailed together.' The authors nevertheless had the grace to add that 'this 5953cc monster is comfortably the equal of anything to have emerged from Maranello or Sant'Agata.' (Maranello was of course the home of Ferrari, and Sant'Agata that of Lamborghini.)

THE TRANSMISSION

In the DB7, Aston Martin had chosen a five-speed ZF automatic gearbox and a six-speed Tremec manual type as the options with the V12 engine; for the Vanquish in 2001, the standard fit was a clutchless manual that did not meet with universal acceptance. For the DB9, the decision was to offer both manual and automatic options, though of course the final choices were made from the most recently introduced, state-of-the-art transmission designs.

To provide optimum weight distribution in the new VH structure, the engineers decided to mount the gearbox over the rear axle, where it would be driven by a lightweight carbon-fibre shaft that ran inside a torque tube cast from aluminium. However, in practice the automatic gearbox chosen weighed some 60kg (132lb) more than its manual

Most DB9s would be built with a six-speed automatic gearbox, of which this is a cutaway model. The alternative was a six-speed manual type.

This ghosted picture gives a further idea of the layout of ZF's 6HP26 automatic gearbox.

counterpart, and was therefore mounted nearer the centre of the car to achieve the correct balance.

For the manual gearbox option, the engineers' choice fell upon a six-speed type of conventional design that was manufactured by Graziano Trasmissioni, a specialist supplier of race-car transmissions, with its British headquarters at St Neots in Cambridgeshire. For the automatic, experience with the five-speed ZF gearbox (with Touchtronic paddle-shift controls) in the DB7 had been positive, and by the time Aston Martin were looking for an automatic suitable for the DB9, ZF were ready with a new six-speed type. So in this case, their choice fell on the latest 6HP26 gearbox – the prefix indicates six-speed, hydraulic converter, planetary geartrain – that was rated to handle 443lb ft (600Nm) of torque. With an electronic shift-by-wire control system and paddle-shift controls on the steering wheel, this would be brought to market and again used the Aston Martin designation of Touchtronic.

SUSPENSION, STEERING AND BRAKES

The suspension arrangement was essentially similar to that on the Vanquish, with double wishbones at all four corners of the car, and steel coils as the springing medium. The front end was designed with anti-dive geometry, and the rear end had dual-rate coil springs and both anti-squat and anti-lift geometry, all features intended to keep the car level under the fierce acceleration and fierce braking that its eventual owners would inevitably use. There were anti-roll bars both front and rear to resist body roll in cornering, and the dampers chosen were monotube adaptive types.

Wheel sizes were gradually increasing as tyre manufacturers developed tyres with ever-shallower sidewalls. An 18in size was standard on the DB7, and a 19in size was the option, and the choice of a 19in size as standard for the DB9 was more or less inevitable. To provide maximum cornering stability and traction for acceleration, the rear wheels were an inch wider than those at the front. Bridgestone was chosen as the original equipment tyre supplier, and the tyres were from their Potenza range, which was known for precision handling and excellent responsiveness. A 235 width was chosen for the front wheels with a 40 per cent aspect ratio, while the wider rear wheels had 275 tyres with a 35 per cent aspect ratio.

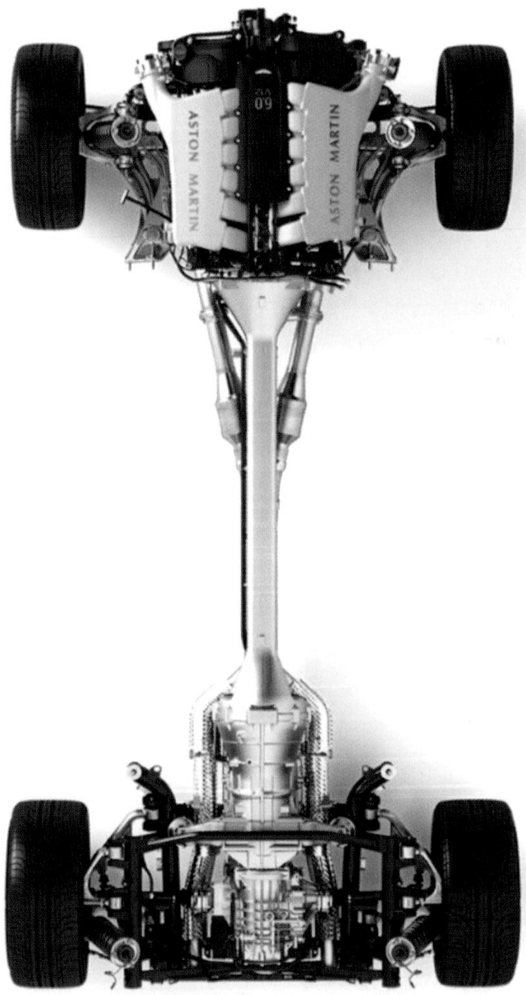

The powertrain of the DB9 was laid out to provide the best possible weight distribution; note the rear-mounted gearbox assembly.

The choice of steering system was straightforward, and the car was brought to production with a rack-and-pinion system that featured hydraulic power assistance. For braking, the choice fell upon four-piston callipers and ventilated discs produced by Brembo, which by this time had become the acknowledged leader in braking hardware. The front discs had a larger 355mm diameter than the rears, which measured 330mm, and there were separate callipers for the handbrake. The standard discs were of course steel, but by the start of the 2000s Brembo was preparing to make carbon ceramic discs available (and first supplied them for the 2002 Ferrari Enzo). Aston Martin had no option but to follow the trend, and therefore made the new technology available as an extra-cost option from the start of DB9 production.

EXTERIOR STYLING

When work began on the shape of the DB9, Aston Martin still had no full-time styling department of its own, and once again the decision was made to commission a design from TWR at Kidlington. Besides, it made good sense to assure design continuity by having it done by the same man who had been responsible for the Vanquish – Ian Callum, the Chief Designer and General Manager of TWR's design studio.

For Callum, this was a very busy period. In 1999, after the untimely death of Jaguar's chief stylist Geoff Lawson, Callum had to juggle design responsibilities for both Aston Martin and Jaguar for a time before eventually moving across to Jaguar on a full-time basis. In the period between 2000 and 2001 he was asked to work on two new Aston Martin designs, and alongside the DB9 he started work on one that would become the V8 Vantage in 2005. Much of this work was done at the Jaguar design centre in Whitley, with assistance from Wayne Burgess.

Both Aston Martin designs were well under way by the time the brand appointed Henrik Fisker as its own dedicated Design Director in 2001, allowing Callum to devote his full attention to Jaguar models. Although the DB9 was finished under Fisker, the basic shape was certainly done by Callum. In an interview with *Car and Driver* magazine in 2010, he was asked how much of the DB9 had been designed on his watch. 'I'd say pretty much 100 per cent,' he answered, 'including the interior. Maybe not colour and trim and wood finishes, but certainly the surfaces of the car.'

Despite such a clear and categorical statement of what happened, there remains some confusion on this issue, and that confusion was initiated at the DB9's launch in 2003. By then, Callum was well established as the high-profile Design Director for Jaguar, and Fisker was equally well established at the helm of Aston Martin. Understandably it was therefore

The body-coloured 'bar' across the rear lights was one of the details added by Henrik Fisker to the initial design by Ian Callum.

Fisker who handled questions about the car at the media launch, and this left many journalists with the impression that he was claiming authorship of its shape. However, it is more likely that he had been asked by Aston Martin management to say as little as possible about Callum's involvement, and chose to focus on the features he had designed himself, such as the body-colour dividing bar across the rear lights. To summarise, the DB9 was Callum's work, modified late in the process by Fisker.

As brought to production readiness, the DB9 style not only seemed like a logical continuation of Ian Callum's style for the DB7 and the V12 Vanquish, but was also very much a modern interpretation of the shapes that had been so much admired on the DB4, DB5 and DB6 models of the 1950s and 1960s. The Aston Martin press release at the DB9's launch in 2003 described it as 'a contemporary version of classic DB design elements and characteristics'. These classic elements and characteristics had been established by the great Italian design house of Carrozzeria Touring, based in Milan, who had been contracted to provide shapes for the cars, and the timeless long-nose, sleek fastback style that they drew up was an obvious influence on the Ian Callum design.

Like its predecessors, the DB9 would have a short protruding boot at the rear, but this would be less immediately obvious and blended into the sloping rear of the passenger cabin. A version of the classic Aston Martin grille was only to be expected, but the prominent bumpers that had characterised those classic designs were no longer in fashion, and instead both front and rear bumpers were blended into the body panels.

Engine-bay air outlets just behind the front wheels were another carryover from the classic Aston Martin designs, with bright metal strakes that reached back across the leading edge of each door. Yet the overall design was very clean, depending on shape rather than ornamentation for its effect. Sculpted sills gave interest to the sides, while both front and rear lights were blended smoothly into the lines of the body.

Then, of course, there was the question of wheel design. Aston Martin doubtless realised that whatever they came up with, it would not prevent aftermarket companies from

DESIGN DIRECTION: HENRIK FISKER

Around three years before the DB9 was put into production, Aston Martin appointed Danish-born Henrik Fisker as Design Director.

Henrik Fisker became Aston Martin Design Director in 2001, and added some final details to the Ian Callum design. This picture was taken some years later, in 2016.

Fisker took up his new appointment in 2001, taking over from Ian Callum, who was juggling responsibilities for both Jaguar and Aston Martin marques at the time. It was Fisker who saw Callum's design for the DB9 through to production, adding a few touches of his own on the way. Among these was the body-coloured bar that splits the tail-light units horizontally and runs across the back end of the car.

Between 1999 and 2001, Fisker had been President and CEO of BMW's DesignWorks studios in California. He then joined the Ford group to oversee Aston Martin design, and between 2001 and 2003 he was also the Creative Director of Ingeni, Ford's forward design centre in London. From August that year, he was appointed Director of Ford's Global Advanced Design Studio at Irvine in California.

He nevertheless continued to oversee design at Aston Martin until 2005, when he stunned his colleagues by announcing that he was leaving to set up Fisker Coachbuild in California, together with Bernhard Koehler, a colleague from BMW and latterly Aston Martin. He subsequently founded Fisker Automotive, and after that Fisker Incorporated, which focused on the development of electric vehicles.

THE FAMILY RESEMBLANCE

Those who are not very familiar with modern Aston Martin models sometimes argue that the DB9 is almost indistinguishable from the V12 Vanquish. The two cars are rarely seen side by side, and this does not help the casual onlooker to identify points of reference that distinguish one from the other. It is only to be expected that there should be a family resemblance between them, but, as with all family resemblances, a closer look reveals the differences. To help convince unbelievers, the two cars are shown together in the pictures that accompany this panel.

Starting at the front end, note how the turn signals of the DB9 are incorporated within the headlight glasses, while those of the Vanquish are let into the front apron; the DB9 has three air intakes in its front apron below the grille, while the Vanquish has a single horizontal slot. Then the sculpting of the side panels is quite different between the two cars.... There are no prizes for completing the list, but it is quite a long one!

For comparison, this is the 2001 Vanquish model...

...and this is the 2003 DB9 Coupé. The family resemblance was close, but a direct comparison between the two cars reveals how different they really were.

developing alternatives that would allow DB9 owners to personalise their cars. The important thing was to provide a design that would be good enough to discourage this. The simple production design with five paired spokes fitted the bill superbly.

There was a satisfying continuity in the new DB9 body's extensive use of aluminium, as the body panels of those classic earlier DB Astons had been made of aluminium-magnesium alloy, which in their case was clenched over an inner structure of small-diameter steel tubes. For the DB9, the bonnet, roof and rear wings would be made of aluminium, while the front wings, front bumper and the boot lid would be of composite construction.

INTERIOR AND PASSENGER CABIN

The DB9 was intended from the outset to be a two-seater design, with plenty of comfort and opulence for two people but little more than token space in the rear of the passenger cabin, which would be more commonly used as a stowage area. Yet there were marketing issues to be considered as well: some buyers wanted to see swathes of padded leather behind the front seats, and not a simple luggage platform, however practical it might be. So a pair of suitably opulent rear seats was designed and made available as an extra-cost option. They were strictly impractical for anyone over the age of about five, but then practicality was not the point, and when the car went on sale it was offered as either a quaintly named (and standard) '2+0', or a 2+2.

The interior design certainly drew on the one that had been designed for the Vanquish, and the newer car repeated the feature of a central stack that was typically trimmed to stand out from the rest of the dashboard. Yet there were many differences, not the least being the way the stack on the DB9 blended into the transmission tunnel. The air vents were mounted lower down, too, leaving space for a pop-up satellite navigation system above them. The arrangement of the switchgear was quite different except for the row of five round controls that were roughly level with the steering wheel's side spokes. Here, the designers avoided the big red central starter button of the Vanquish that some had considered rather vulgar, and instead had settled for an almost bijou piece of design. The DB9 solution was a clear glass starter button that was etched with the Aston Martin logo. With the ignition on, the button glowed blue, and that colour turned to red when the engine was running.

Well aware that earlier Aston Martins had been criticised for their use of switchgear and other items borrowed from lesser cars, for the DB9 the company did its best to make everything the customer saw or touched unique to Aston Martin. Their efforts were not wholly successful – and accusations of parts borrowing would later be levelled at the DB9's interior – but they did develop a new 'corporate' switch that could be adapted for multiple functions and simply labelled appropriately. Behind the bespoke items, much of the electrical architecture and many of the electronic modules were borrowed from Volvo, although programmed where appropriate to Aston Martin requirements. The infotainment system depended on fibre optics and a MOST (media-orientated system transportation) system that was also based on Volvo originals, although the Linn sound system chosen for production was specially designed for the DB9.

As signed off for production, the interior had a very distinct style of its own, with a relatively plain expanse of dashboard ahead of the front-seat occupants, and that attractively symmetrical centre stack that swept down to a console between the seats. On DB9s with the automatic transmission, four buttons on the centre stack selected the traditional P-R-N-D positions electrically, and of course the steering wheel featured paddle-shifts to give the driver more direct control over the gearshifts.

A further option developed for the launch was a seating package that replaced the standard front seats with lightweight items made from Kevlar and carbon fibre, and came with the rear luggage platform rather than the '+2' seats. Its main advantage was weight saving (and a secondary one was, of course, bragging rights), and inevitably it was an expensive extra.

TESTING AND PROTOTYPES

The DB9 prototypes were put through an extremely rigorous test programme that saw a cumulative total of a million miles driven in a multitude of locations. Ford-owned facilities played their part, and a great deal of testing was carried out at the Lommel proving ground in Belgium, supplemented by high-speed work at the independently owned Nardo track in Italy and at the Nürburgring in Germany. There was work at both the MIRA and Millbrook test tracks in the UK. Crash testing was carried out at the then-new Volvo crash-test safety centre at Torslanda, near Gothenburg in Sweden.

For hot-weather testing, the cars went to Death Valley, one of the hottest places on earth and located on the inland side of California in the USA. Then for cold-weather work, the location was once again Sweden, this time within the Arctic Circle in the very north of the country. Further summer and winter tests were carried out in New Zealand.

Most of the test cars were later destroyed, but three survived and were used in the 2007 James Bond 007 film, *Casino Royale*. Aston Martin supplied two standard DBS models for use in the close-up sequences, plus a white DB9 prototype for the film crew and stunt driver to practise the rollover that was intended to end a spectacular car-chase sequence. In addition, two more DB9 development cars were modified to look like the new DBS and to be sacrificed in the film sequences.

The film cars were all finished in the same dark silver-grey, and all wore the (false) number plate TT 378 20. The filming was done one afternoon during 2006 at the Millbrook Vehicle Proving Ground near Bedford, and the two sacrificial cars were put through a high-speed rollover for the cameras. This was achieved with the aid of a 30cm (18in) ramp on the road and an air-assisted ram built into each car behind the driver's seat. The plan was to use the best footage from each rollover in the eventual film, but there was no contest about the outcome. In the hands of stunt driver Adam Kirley, one of the cars rolled no fewer than seven times while travelling at more than 113km/h (70mph), shedding panels in spectacular fashion during a quite thrilling 30 seconds or so of footage, and also setting a new world record that was duly listed in the Guinness Book of Records.

Not surprisingly, not one of those three cars survived the experience to be driven again – but they did help to maintain the link between the James Bond film franchise and Aston Martin that had played such a large part in the marque's revival in the mid-1960s.

CHAPTER 6

THE EARLY DB9, 2003–2008

It is hard to keep secrets in the motor industry, and Aston Martin engineers were probably not surprised to read in the issue of *Autocar* dated 21 August 2002 that they were working on a 'New Aston DB7'. Although it was not going to be called a DB7, the new car was certainly destined to replace the DB7, and quite a lot of the commentary around the *Autocar* scoop was accurate. Nevertheless, the official launch was still a year away.

That launch was more in the nature of a preview, because the new Aston Martin had not actually entered production by the time it was displayed to the public at the Frankfurt Motor Show that opened in early September 2003. The pre-production model displayed on the Aston Martin stand nevertheless drew its fair share of attention at a show that hosted no fewer than 125 world premières.

Aston representatives promised more news later, along with a proper media launch event, but one key question that occurred to many of the media at Frankfurt concerned the name of the new car. The last new Aston had been called a DB7, so why was this one not called a DB8? There was

The sleek and beautiful shape of the DB9 was a strong factor in its appeal, as this early white demonstrator shows.

Silver was always a favourite colour for the DB9, and it certainly brought out the lines to perfection. This LHD car was delivered to an owner in France.

The rear spoiler was neatly integrated into the overall lines of the body. This rear view illustrates the overall harmony of the lines penned by Ian Callum.

a ready answer to this, and Aston claimed that there were two reasons. One was that the car had a V12 engine, and that the name of DB8 would have suggested that it was a V8. The other, perhaps a little more disingenuous, was that the company considered the DB8 name would have suggested a gradual evolution from the DB7, whereas the new car was in fact a radical departure from what had gone before and deserving of a more complete break with past model names!

Dark colours gave the DB9 a very different appearance, and arguably made it stand out a little less than light ones.

Volume production began at Aston Martin's new factory in Gaydon in January 2004, and a number of the first cars were earmarked for the media launch. This was held during February in the south of France and was based on a hotel situated right on the fast, twisting road that leads to the Col de Vence. Amusingly, Ferrari had planned to launch their new 612 Scaglietti coupé on the very same Monday at a venue in Italy. Somebody had to back down, and it was Ferrari who did, moving the date of their media launch to the previous Friday. The change meant that a good percentage of the journalists from around the world who had been tasked to report on both new cars came to the Aston Martin launch with their senses still full of the Ferrari's excellence. It was going to be a hard act for Aston Martin to follow – although there was, of course, a very big difference in the list prices of the two cars.

WHAT THE PRESS THOUGHT

The DB9 launch was the biggest event of its type that Aston Martin had ever hosted, and it went extremely well. It also generated some very positive coverage in both newspapers and the specialist motoring press. Some reports were quite euphoric, and must very quickly have confirmed to Aston Martin that their initial plan to build 1,400–1,500 DB9s a year might have to be revised – upwards. However, it was very noticeable that in later years, as some of those who tried early DB9s looked back on the experience, they did not remember it quite as fondly. That early euphoria seems to have been enough to allow some of the less positive aspects of the cars to go unremarked, at least in print.

'Taken as a whole, the DB9 is a masterpiece and an Aston that finally fulfils the promise of its looks,' said Andrew Frankel in *The Sunday Times* of 14 March. Writing in the same newspaper for 18 April, Jeremy Clarkson described the car as 'perfect... like everything mankind knows about excitement and machinery and technology has finally come together in an orgasm of absolute, thrilling and total harmony.'

Meanwhile, *The Daily Telegraph* motoring supplement dated 27 March remarked on the transformation that the new car represented:

> *Not long ago, before the Ford takeover (and even for a while afterwards), buying an Aston Martin was a commitment for the ultra-rich and slightly eccentric. Some of those hand-built cars were very good in their own way, but they were costly to run, fragile, and impractical for everyday use. That has all changed. The new Astons are precisely the cars that*

> *previous owners of the company… could only dream of building. It might have taken a German [that is, Ulrich Bez] to do it, but Aston Martin has brilliantly reinvented itself, moving boldly into the modern era while retaining the essence of the company's tradition.*

The hugely influential weekly *Autocar* magazine arranged a group test in time for their issue dated 16 March, pitting the new Aston against a Lamborghini Gallardo and a Porsche 911 Turbo (with power kit). They voted the DB9 as better than either, concluding that its 'killer punch lies in its ability to place that blend of performance, handling and exquisite cabin ambience within the context of Aston Martin, the brand. It's a deeply compelling package.'

Evo magazine, having a longer lead time, did not report on the new Aston until its May 2004 issue, which of course reached the shops in late April. Their summary was also hugely positive: 'Aston Martin hasn't just succeeded in building the best car in its history; on this evidence it has built the most complete, accomplished, involving and seductively styled car in the world.'

Autocar contrived to feature the DB9 again in their issue of 1 June 2004, and this time gave it the full road-test treatment. In terms of hard figures, they reported a 0–60mph acceleration time of 5.4sec and a 13.7sec standing-start quarter-mile, which were very respectable results. They suggested that there was 'not much that will out-drag a DB9 in a straight line', and were generally very impressed with the whole car, awarding it four and a half stars out of a possible five overall.

Details matter: the mesh side vents picked up on past Aston Martin styling, while the side repeater lenses were clear to suit multiple different body colours, but concealed amber bulbs to meet traffic regulations.

This underbonnet view shows how the 6.0-litre V12 engine was presented to look attractive as well as to impress.

The model badging at the rear was discreet but unmistakable, with the '9' hanging stylishly below the DB letters.

Branding was quite discreet. The Aston Martin name was not displayed in large letters on the tail, but instead the company's winged logo was positioned in the centre.

The sill plates left no room for doubt about what the car was once a door was opened, or about where it had been made.

'There isn't a better drivetrain on sale,' they said, and although they thought the DB9 was very firmly sprung by conventional standards, 'it remains a fine blend of comfort and agility.' Though agile for its size, it was not a car that could be 'threaded' as easily as a Porsche 911, but the testers did admire its handling balance. They detected a touch of understeer, but this was more than matched by grip levels so high that 'in the dry, only the insane will try and find where it finally ends.'

There was not much to criticise. The steering was too heavy, the ride was rather choppy, and a few of the dashboard switches were a let-down in such an expensive car. The overall conclusion was that this was a car that was 'extraordinarily desirable and supremely capable', and that it was 'the best car Aston Martin has ever made, and a tantalising preview of what's to come from Gaydon.'

Almost a year to the day after that major road test, *Autocar* borrowed another DB9, this time with the Graziano manual gearbox rather than the ZF automatic. In the issue dated 14 June 2005, they quoted Aston Martin as telling them that the company's cars 'have always appealed to the more discerning sports-car drivers, to the sorts of drivers who like to change gear manually,' and that this was why a manual gearbox was always planned as an option for the DB9. In practice, it appears that the company was struggling at this stage to keep up with demand for the automatic models, and that somebody had decided that a little positive publicity for the manual variants (which were, of course, less expensive) might provide a partial solution.

The silver face panel of the sweeping centre stack contrasts strongly with the black principal colour in the interior of this LHD model. The panel at the top of the stack is for the pop-up satellite navigation screen.

Colour choice made a big difference to the feel of the interior. In this case, the leather trim is a dark red, but still lighter than the black in the picture above.

Aston Martin took great pride in the amount of hand-building that went into every DB9. Every V12 engine carried a plate with the name of the man who had built it.

Autocar thought that the Graziano gearbox was much better than the manual option in the old DB7, which they described as notchy and slow-shifting. They also questioned the official claim that the manual DB9 was only 0.1sec quicker to 60mph than the automatic. 'In reality, it's quite a lot faster than the auto and no mistake,' they said, adding that the manual car 'has the feel of a genuinely incisive sports car, and that's something you could never quite say with a straight face about the automatic.'

Perhaps there was a feeling that early press reports on the DB9 had been too effusive, because it was not long before the negative comments began to appear. There had been some mildly snide remarks since the beginning, such as the observation that the key was actually an old Jaguar item, but now the negative criticism intensified.

Evo magazine was one of the early naysayers, and its August 2004 comparison test of a DB9 with a Bentley Continental GT and a Porsche 911 Turbo highlighted just where the Aston fell short. 'There's a great car locked inside the DB9,' they said. 'On paper it's a winner, with its advanced aluminium superstructure, front-mid-engine/transaxle layout, glorious engine and superb gearbox. The driving experience simply doesn't reflect this, though, which is immensely frustrating.' One member of the test team explained his feelings about the car with the words, 'Somehow it doesn't feel finished yet.'

Evo's main criticisms were of the steering and the suspension:

> *It's not just steering weight but response, too. On the fast, smooth section of our route the DB9 feels OK, but although it corners with strong grip and a roll-free attitude, there isn't the feeling that the Aston turns enthusiastically, or that its chassis flows naturally into and out of a corner. Throw in a few moderate undulations, and the Aston becomes even less satisfying. It seems unable to cope with single-wheel bumps, the whole front end rocking over them, and the odd thing is that despite its substantial extruded aluminium chassis, the DB9 seems to flex over rough tarmac. All of which makes trying to exploit the long-legged urge of its howling V12 rather frustrating. We want to love the DB9 but the way it drives won't let us. As it stands, it's neither a great cruiser nor a confidence-inspiring driver's GT.*

Car magazine, traditionally hard-hitting, prefaced a review in August 2006 by saying that 'the DB9 has always been a great looking car but sadly it's never been as good to drive as to look at. The ride was too crashy for a GT, the throttle too aggressive, it was a handful in the wet and skipped over bumps.' (That same review nevertheless enthusiastically noted that the DB9 'sounds fantastic from the moment the revs flare up at the press of the starter button and even better when the exhaust valve opens half way up the rev range.')

Finely sculpted details for the electric window switches and the door pulls added immeasurably to the interior ambience.

Even the leather-bound owner's manual was a minor work of art.

This commemorative plaque was issued at an Aston Martin Owners' Club meeting at Silverstone in 2004, which celebrated the outgoing DB7 and welcomed the new DB9.

Some four years later, it was again in *Car* magazine, this time dated 17 June 2010, that Tim Pollard said, 'I remember driving one of the very first DB9s back in 2003, and while the style and V12 oomph blew me away, I was surprisingly disappointed by the build quality. The leather-clad interior was roughly finished in places and some of the controls wobbled and rattled.' And *Autocar* of 31 August 2015 (at about the time the last DB9s were being made) recalled that 'when it was launched, the DB9 had plastic switches to move the seats, and the Volvo-sourced satellite navigation system was rubbish even then.'

ENTER THE VOLANTE

The first DB9s for customers in the UK reached their new owners in spring 2004, and the cars went on sale in the USA over the summer of that year. Aston Martin were already making minor adjustments to the specification, although these were not advertised. Some of those who had attended the media launch nevertheless noted that the adjustable dampers on the launch cars had not been carried over to the production models. The rather aggressive throttle response of the first automatics was also toned down to give a more controllable feel.

A convertible alternative to the DB9 coupé had been planned right from the start of the DB9 project, and the whole VH structure had been designed and engineered with such a variation in mind. Production of the DB9 Volante began at Gaydon a year after that of the coupé, and the car's makers had high hopes of its sales. They expected the Volante to account for around half of all DB9s sold, and for no less than 70 per cent of DB9s sold in the critically important US market, even though the convertible variant would be more expensive than the coupé. This latter statistic no doubt influenced the decision to announce the DB9 Volante at the Detroit Auto Show in the USA in January 2004.

The Volante came with the same engine and transmission options as the DB9 coupé, but its structure had been stiffened to compensate for the absence of a fixed roof and as a result the convertible model was quite noticeably heavier than the coupé at 1,880kg (4,150lb). There were strengthened windscreen pillars, and a pair of pop-up hoops behind the rear seats provided rollover protection (they would also punch through the rear window if the soft top was erected). Additional stiffening came from slightly thicker aluminium in the sill sections, and from a shear panel that was bolted to the underside and covered most of the front half of the car.

The suspension had also been retuned, with softer springs all round, less restrictive anti-roll bars, and softer damping. The changes were partly made to match the increased weight, but they also had the effect of changing the car's character. Well over a year after the Volante's introduction, *Autocar* of 24 May 2005 summed it up as 'more than just a roofless coupé: it's really a whole new model, developed with a different kind of Aston buyer in mind. A DB9 engineer used the ungainly phrase "boulevard cruiser", but it gives you the idea.' As if that different kind of Aston buyer needed to be reminded, when the ignition key was turned, a moving dot matrix in the rev counter presented the message 'Power, Beauty, Soul'.

The convertible roof was concealed under a tonneau cover when not in use, but could be raised in just 17sec. The operation was fully automatic, and was triggered by a switch on the centre console. When raised, the roof had a beautiful fit and sleek lines that were entirely in keeping with the DB9's shape and pretensions, and perhaps the only real disadvantage was that its mechanism took up a noticeable

The DB9 styling worked supremely well in Volante convertible form, as this early example demonstrates.

The Volante retained all the grace and sleekness of the coupé from which it was derived.

The folding roof of a convertible can make or break the styling when it is erected. The one on the Volante worked extremely well, as this Monaco-registered example shows.

This rear view of the same car shows the finely judged lines of the soft top, and its wide if shallow rear window. The centre brake light with its clear lens can be seen just above the Aston Martin logo.

An open Volante on a twisty coast road in fine weather – the ideal car for the conditions.

section of the boot space. The Volante's boot volume was 136ltr (4.8cu ft) as against the DB9 coupé's 187ltr (6.6cu ft). The convertible model's top speed was also limited to 266km/h (165mph) in order to protect the integrity of the roof – but not many owners were going to drive the cars hard enough to find that out.

The already impressive DB9 interior remained unchanged, with its soft and supple leather supplied by Bridge of Weir in as many as twenty different colours, and the option of bamboo, mahogany or walnut wood trims. For maximum clarity the gauges were floodlit, while the trip computer had an electro-luminescent display to give maximum resolution. There was no chance of failing to hear music clearly at high speeds in this open car, thanks to a standard ICE system (made by Linn) that delivered up to 950 watts of sound and benefited from a 200-watt sub-woofer.

In an assessment published by *Autocar* in May 2005, Adam Towler gave the car a very careful appraisal: 'Safe to say,' he wrote, 'if you're thinking of ordering one you'll need to be an exhibitionist who loves to bask in the attention of others, and I guess that's an acquired taste.' Yet the DB9 Volante was not by any means brash or vulgar. 'Without resorting to any retro cheesiness, it completely avoids the shock tactics that some manufacturers deem necessary to create visual impact. It simply looks magnificent: a blend of British power, prestige, athleticism and gilt-edged affluence to steal the show anywhere in the world.'

It was also impressive to drive, with 'heavy steering and brake pedal, firm ride and excellent gearbox – a proper slusher, but with an uncannily good paddle-shift function complete with throttle blips on downchanges.' Towler was nevertheless not keen on the fly-off handbrake, which he found 'occasionally awkward'. He also provided an excellent impression of what the car was like to drive:

> *One of the odd sensations you get driving a DB9 – magnified in the Volante – is how much car is in front of you and how much inertia you have to overcome before you can really turn into a corner. You sit low, with acres of dashboard stretching out in front of you*

and a mass of bonnet after that, hidden from view. As such, the car seems to pivot from a point some way ahead of the driver's seat, and you're always aware in slower corners of the weight of the V12 up front. The steering is heavy initially, but once you've turned into a corner the car feels as if it's understeering early and in a pronounced way, only to regain its composure and grip keenly around a corner from there on.

A few more road tests in the years that followed ensured that the DB9 Volante would remain in the consciousness of potential buyers, but not all of them were wholly complimentary. In *The Sunday Times* dated 20 May 2007, the car was described as 'gorgeous but dynamically compromised', and the writer insisted that 'the DB9 coupé is a wildly better car to drive than the Volante.'

It was very much a case of horses for courses, and just as happened with the coupé, the Volante suffered in later years from its fair share of negative memories that seem to have been largely suppressed when the cars were new. An example was in *Car* magazine of 18 May 2011, when one writer remembered driving a 2004 Volante: 'I hit a bump,' he said. 'Maybe two. The structure buzzed like a tuning fork, the suspension clattered loudly, the body floated and crashed uncomfortably and the glamour disappeared with a resounding thud. The next few miles were perplexing and disappointing. The DB9 Volante was a bit of a mess.'

ADDING THE SPORTS PACK

Just as the makers of everyday family saloons keep customer interest alive by introducing attractive new features at regular intervals, so the makers of a supercar such as the DB9 like to tempt their customers with novelties. The main difference is that those customers are in a position to pay more than the buyer of an everyday family model, and that the new features can be correspondingly more exotic and expensive. A favourite trick is to introduce a feature that can be sold as an 'upgrade' to an existing car.

This kind of thinking was very much behind the next change to the DB9 range. The original coupé had gone on sale in January 2004, the Volante had followed it in January 2005, and now in October 2006 Aston Martin introduced the Sports Pack option. It was available on newly ordered cars or as an 'upgrade' to a customer's vehicle, but only on coupés; there was no Sports Pack for the Volante models.

The Sports Pack was essentially a reworked suspension system, with minor changes that (claimed Aston Martin) improved body control and maintained a neutral handling

MAREK REICHMAN

After Henrik Fisker left Aston Martin in early 2005, the company appointed Marek Reichman as its new Director of Design with effect from May that year. Reichman oversaw subsequent development of the DB9 design.

Born in Sheffield in 1966, Reichman had an English mother and a Polish father. He was the first student on the Royal College of Art's Vehicle Design course to be sponsored by Land Rover, and in 1991 he took up a first appointment with Rover Cars. After BMW bought the Rover and Land Rover marques in 1994, Reichman moved to the BMW DesignWorks studio in California. Here he contributed to advanced design concepts, including the forthcoming third-generation Range Rover.

Reichman moved to Ford in 1999, where he was appointed Chief Designer for the company's Ford and Lincoln Mercury brands, later rising to the position of Director of Design for Product at Ford North America. When the vacancy arose at Aston Martin, he was moved across to the brand's headquarters in Britain.

Marek Reichman took over as Aston Martin Design Director in summer 2005 and had responsibility for the later visual and interior changes.

balance, all the while having no impact on the quality of the DB9's ride. The ride was certainly stiffer, and perhaps that was why the Sports Pack was made available only for the coupé models: the convertible structure might have shown its reduced rigidity over bumps with the harder suspension. Ride height was reduced by 6mm, spring rates were increased by 68 per cent at the front and 64 per cent at the rear, while a fatter front anti-roll bar was also part of the package, along with uprated dampers and modified bump-stops. For good measure, a new load-bearing aluminium panel replaced the composite airflow-management under-tray to cope with the greater loads that the revised front suspension fed into the structure.

This was serious business, but of course Aston Martin knew very well that a proportion of potential buyers would want to have the Sports Pack simply because it was the latest thing – some cultures think of such features as conferring 'bragging rights' on the owner – and for those buyers the handling benefits were of little consequence. Much more important was that the presence of the Sports Pack could be advertised in some way.

The obvious way of doing this was to make a set of distinctive wheels part of the package, and Aston Martin did so. The Sports Pack wheels were forged alloy types, each one 1kg (2.2lb) lighter than a standard wheel, and with a most attractive design featuring five paired alloy spokes. On their own, and without the Sports Pack suspension, these wheels became available as a cosmetic upgrade for the Volante models as well. On early cars they came with special titanium wheel nuts that were visually different from the standard type. It was quite true that these nuts were also lighter than the standard type, but it would be a rare customer who noticed any difference when driving the car, and in fairness the greatest benefit of the special nuts lay in the bragging rights department.

So saying, *Car* magazine in August 2006 thought that the ride offered by the Sports Pack was actually better than the standard car's, and that the steering seemed to offer more feel.

The Sports Pack certainly did not impress everyone. Writing in *Octane* magazine for January 2020, John Simister recalled his first drive in a manual DB9 with the sports suspension package. 'It was not nice at all,' he said, 'with a fidgety, thumpy ride, lots of road roar and the feeling of a great car ruined. Its manual transmission was tetchy, too, in that co-ordinating a narrow bite-band clutch and a hard-to-modulate throttle made gentle driving far harder than it should have been.'

THE 2007 MODELS

The Sports Pack may have been the headline change for the 2007 model-year, but it was far from being the only one. Several changes were made to the mainstream production models, and among them were improvements to the

The Sports Pack came with its own special wheels, as seen here on a DB9 coupé.

The centre stack of this Volante shows the revised layout of the 2007 models.

electrical components to improve reliability. One upgrade carried out before the end of 2006 was to the V12 engine's coil packs, when the original two-wire type was replaced by a three-wire type. The precise point at which the change was made is nevertheless not clear, and Aston Martin themselves have admitted that they do not know exactly when it occurred!

Other changes for 2007 included a new design of front seat, while the door handles were now equipped with LED approach lights. Meanwhile the speed restrictor applied to the early DB9 Volante models was removed, no doubt because enough customers had complained that there was no threat to the integrity of the convertible roof if that roof were safely stowed in its well when they chose to exceed 256km/h (165mph)! So the 2007 and later models of the Volante were theoretically capable of the full 299km/h (186mph) that the coupé models could achieve.

THE DB9 LM SPECIAL EDITION, 2008

Meanwhile, as Chapter 7 explains, Aston Martin had embarked on a racing programme with the DBR9 derivative of the DB9 coupé, and in June 2007 had achieved victory in the GT1 category of the Le Mans 24 Hours endurance race. The promotional benefits of this success were rapidly exploited by a celebratory special edition that was announced at the Frankfurt Motor Show in the autumn, for sale as a 2008 model.

The DB9 LM special edition was not made available immediately, but went on sale in the first quarter of 2008, and customer deliveries were made in February and March of that year. In effect, it became a run-out model for the early DB9. Aston Martin originally planned to build up to 124 examples – one for each of the company's dealers – but

The 2008 Le Mans special edition celebrated the Aston Martin GT1 victory at Le Mans. This example was pictured in Hong Kong.

The Le Mans edition had the Sports Pack as standard, with these 19in diamond-turned five-spoke wheels.

A map of the Sarthe circuit was added on this red plaque next to the DB9 emblem on the Le Mans special-edition cars.

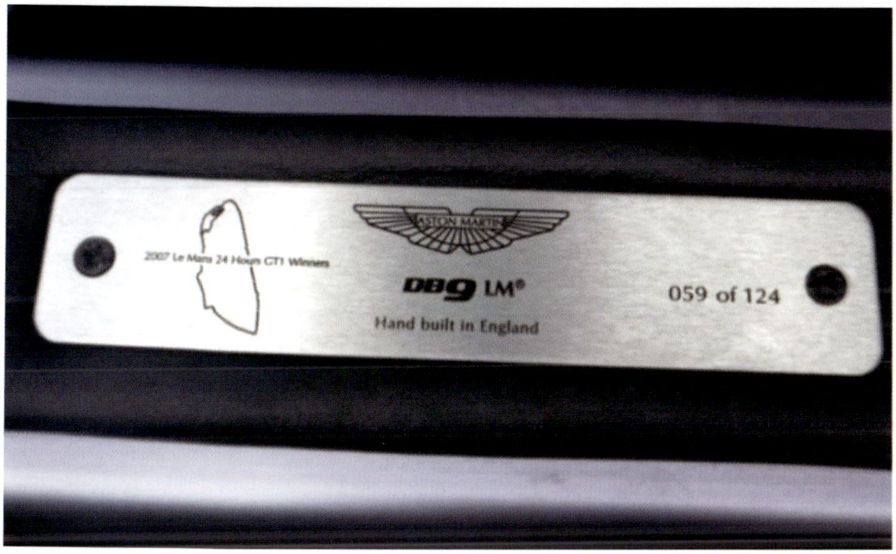

The sill plates of the Le Mans celebration cars carried each car's individual number within the special edition.

demand for the car did not support that and a much lower quantity was actually built. The generally accepted figure is 69 cars. Buyers paid a hefty premium for the privilege of owning one: the DB9 LM was priced at £124,000, or €180,000 on the European continent.

All these special-edition cars were coupés with the Touchtronic 2 automatic gearbox – the six-speed Graziano manual was not even offered as an option. All of them had the Sports Pack as standard, and all of them also had some distinctive recognition features.

The only exterior colour available was Sarthe Silver, named after the Circuit de la Sarthe where the Le Mans event is run, a light silver that was instantly recognisable to DB9 *aficionados*, but which was just another variety of silver to the uninitiated. More distinctive were the red-finished brake callipers visible through the 19in diamond-turned five-spoke wheels of the Sports Pack, and the clear rear-lamp lenses that were making their first appearance on a DB9 after being seen on the DBS. Also new and distinctive were the bright Magnum Silver finish for the mesh panels, and the bright front grille. For confirmation, the right-hand side of the tail carried a small red-enamelled badge that was shaped like a map of the Le Mans circuit.

The interior had its own special treatment, with Obsidian Black leather featuring perforated seat inserts and highlighted by bright red stitching to match the brake callipers and tail badge. There was a Le Mans circuit map embroidered in red on the centre arm rest, and the bright red was carried over to create unmissable, vivid feature panels on the centre console and the door cappings. Here, the colour was described as Tertre Rouge, a name taken from a famously sharp corner on the Le Mans circuit. All this was offset by a headlining in either grey or black, and each car carried a sill plate bearing its individual build number within the special edition.

The promise of this special edition at the start of the 2008 model-year was enough to keep sales buoyant without any further changes to the mainstream models. However, Aston Martin were already working on a mid-life facelift for the DB9, and this would be announced in May 2008.

TECHNICAL SPECIFICATIONS: ASTON MARTIN DB9, 2003–2008

Engine
All-alloy V12 with 4 valves per cylinder
5935cc (89mm bore x 79.5 stroke)
Four chain-driven overhead camshafts
Compression ratio 10.3:1
Visteon engine management
450bhp at 6,000rpm
420lb ft at 5,000rpm

Gearbox
ZF 6HP26 six-speed automatic with Touchtronic electronic shift-by-wire control system;
or
Six-speed Graziano Trasmissioni manual.

Axle ratio
3.15:1

Suspension
Front suspension with double wishbones, incorporating anti-dive geometry, coil springs, anti-roll bar and monotube adaptive telescopic dampers.
Rear suspension with double wishbones with anti-squat and anti-lift geometry, dual-rate coil springs, anti-roll bar and monotube adaptive telescopic dampers.

Steering
Rack-and-pinion system with standard power assistance.

Brakes
Ventilated discs on all four wheels, with 355mm diameter at the front and 330mm diameter at the rear; carbon ceramic discs optional.
ABS standard, with Brake Assist and Electronic Brakeforce Distribution; Dynamic Stability Control and traction control.

Wheels and tyres
19in (483mm) alloy wheels with 8.5in (216mm) rims at the front and 9.5in (241mm) rims at the rear.
Bridgestone Potenza RE050 235/40ZR19 tyres (front) and 275/35ZR19 tyres (rear).

Dimensions

Overall length:	4,697mm (184.9in)
Overall width:	2,017mm (79.4in) over mirrors
Overall height:	1,318mm (51.9in)
Wheelbase:	2,740mm (107.9in)
Track, front:	1,568mm (61.7in)
Track, rear:	1,562mm (61.5in)

Kerb weight

1,760kg (3,880lb)	Coupé
1,800kg (3,970lb)	Volante

CHAPTER 7

MOTOR SPORT: THE DBR9 AND DBRS9

The association of Aston Martin with racing was, and remains, an essential element in the marque's story. When the marque was founded in 1913, one of its aims was competition success, and in 1922 it made its international racing debut with two cars entered in the French Grand Prix. The 1929 Aston Martin International model set new standards for handling and road holding, and in 1932 Bertelli and Driscoll won the Biennial Cup at Le Mans.

In the 1940s, it was industrialist David Brown's passion for high-performance cars that persuaded him to buy the Aston Martin company, and he quickly recognised that participation in international racing would help propel the ailing company back to commercial success. The DB1 and DB2 did well in their own class, but it was clear that the success Brown had in mind would only come with a purpose-built sports racer. That car materialised in 1952

The motor-sport tradition: Aston Martin had last won Le Mans in 1959, with this DBR1 sports-racer in the hands of Carroll Shelby and Roy Salvadori.

as the DB3S, which rapidly showed its potential when it entered the globally famous Le Mans 24 Hours event. While customer cars helped to bring in much needed funds, the Aston Martin works team went on to class wins at Le Mans in 1955, 1956 and 1957, hugely enhancing the reputation of the DB3S.

Next came the DBR1, when the Aston Martin works team broke lap records and won no fewer than six world championship races. Their success culminated in a victory in the World Sports Car Championship in 1959 and an outright win at the Le Mans 24 Hours event, when Roy Salvadori and Carroll Shelby in the winning car were followed home by Jean-Louis Trintignant and Paul Frère in second place.

The aura of the marque's golden years of racing lingered for more than four decades, during which the marketing focus moved elsewhere, not least thanks to the massively successful link with the James Bond 007 film franchise. Some of those years were bleak financially for Aston Martin, and the huge cost of an international racing programme was simply beyond reach. However, once the company had the vast resources of Ford behind it, and Ford could see that major investment would not be wasted, the idea of a return to racing gained ground.

So it was that Aston Martin Racing was established in 2004 as a partnership between Aston Martin and leading race-car engineers Prodrive at Banbury in Oxfordshire. Prodrive would actually build the race cars, but Aston Martin would provide the essential elements and would have its own engineering input – and, in time-honoured fashion, it would also be able to take away lessons learned from the race tracks to improve its road cars.

Aston Martin Racing set out with ambitious plans. In the beginning it would return the marque to sports-car racing with an appropriately prepared version of its latest DB9 model, but it was ready to build on the success that it anticipated for this car. The Aston Martin DBR9, named in honour of the earlier DBR1 model, made its debut in 2005 in the GT1 class at the top level of FIA international racing, attracting huge interest and immediately demonstrating a winning ability. By the end of that first year, Aston Martin Racing had announced plans to offer a less expensive DBRS9 model to customer teams who wished to compete at the lower GT3 level of the sport, and a later expansion of plans included a development of the V12 engine for Le Mans prototype use.

AMR as a company would go on to many racing successes in the first quarter of the 21st century, but its foundation was that early success with the cars based on the DB9, and this chapter focuses on that period.

CREATING THE DBR9

The DBR9 was developed specifically to race in the GT1 class of FIA motor-sport events, and there was no doubt that an underlying hope for the programme was a repeat of the DBR1's success at Le Mans in 1959. The cars did achieve success at Le Mans, but that success came in the form of class wins, and there was never an overall victory such as the DBR1 had achieved. Nevertheless, the DBR9 racers achieved their aim of attracting global publicity to the Aston Martin brand, and although Aston Martin Racing switched to other models in 2009, customer teams continued to race them until the GT1 class was ended in 2011.

Fundamental to the development of the DBR9 were modifications to reduce the weight of the road-going DB9 coupé, and in practice the race cars would be a massive 590kg (1,300lb) lighter than the early road cars, with a race weight of just 1,170kg (2,579lb). Key to this light weight was the replacement of almost all the aluminium alloy panels by carbon-fibre equivalents; only the roof remained in aluminium. The luxurious interior was stripped out, and only essential controls and a single lightweight seat were left, while a full race-spec rollover cage was built into the cabin.

Aerodynamics played their part too, and the body was given an underside that was flat all the way from the front apron to the rear diffuser. A front splitter and a carbon-fibre rear wing were added to increase the downforce and therefore the grip at speed. Meanwhile the suspension was respecified for racing, and the standard Brembo four-piston brake callipers gave way to the same manufacturer's six-piston callipers acting on carbon-carbon composite discs.

The drivetrain also went through a major rework. By the time the Prodrive engineers had finished, the engine achieved peak power of 625bhp (as compared to the 540bhp of the road car) with 550lb ft of torque (as against 457lb ft). The standard six-speed ZF automatic gearbox was not at all suitable for racing, despite its undoubted excellence in the road cars, and in its place came a race-bred Xtrac six-speed sequential manual type. A lightweight carbon-fibre propshaft then took the power to a Salisbury friction-plate limited-slip differential. In its initial incarnation, the DBR9 was claimed to accelerate to 60mph (97km/h) in just 3.4sec, while 100mph (160km/h) came up in just 6.4sec.

This basic specification served the DBR9 from 2005 to 2011, but of course there was a process of continuous development to get the best out of the race cars, as is always the case. Changing race regulations also had their impact, and for the 2007 Le Mans entry Prodrive were obliged to install an air-conditioning unit – which the race organisers insisted was intended to reduce driver stress. In practice, they went one better, giving the race cars a white roof to help keep cockpit temperatures down. At the same time, removing a pair of redundant cooling vents from the cars' bonnets probably made a tiny improvement to the aerodynamics.

The prototype of the DBR9 was shown to the media in 2004, and its looks made very clear that Aston Martin were serious about their competition endeavours.

TECHNICAL SPECIFICATIONS: DBR9

These specifications relate to the original 2005 cars.

Engine
V12 with 4 valves per cylinder.
5935cc (89mm bore x 79.5 stroke).
Four chain-driven overhead camshafts.
625bhp (634PS)
550lb ft (746Nm)

Gearbox
X-Trac six-speed sequential manual.

Rear axle
Salisbury limited-slip differential.

Suspension
Twin wishbones on all four wheels, with adjustable Koni dampers.

Steering
Power-assisted rack-and-pinion.

Brakes
Brembo carbon-carbon discs with six-piston callipers.

Dimensions

Overall length:	4,687mm (184.5in)
Overall width:	1,978mm (77.9in)
Overall height:	1,195mm (47.0in)
Wheelbase:	2,741mm (107.9in)
Track, front:	1,568mm (61.7in)
Track, rear:	1,462mm (61.5in)

Weight
1,170kg (2,579lb)

THE TEAMS

The 'works' team of Aston Martin Racing campaigned the DBR9 between 2005 and 2008, and was run by Prodrive. There were also two works-sponsored teams active between 2005 and 2007. These were Aston Martin Racing Larbre and Aston Martin Racing BMS. The Larbre team was based at Le Vigeant in France and was run by Larbre Compétition, while the BMS team was run from Italy by BMS Scuderia Italia.

Some examples of the DBR9 were also sold to private teams and were used in various racing series, especially in the USA where they appeared in the American Le Mans Series. Other appearances were in the Le Mans Series in Europe, the FIA GT Championship, the French FFSA GT Championship and the Japanese Super GT series.

Customer teams that raced the DBR9 were as follows:

Cirtek Racing (later Team Modena)	2005–2008
Phoenix Racing	2006–2007
RaceAlliance (later JetAlliance)	2006–2009
Barwell Motorsports	2007
Gigawave Motorsport	2007–2009
Bell Motorsports	2008
Strakka Racing (as Vitaphone Racing)	2008
Team Nova	2009
Hexis AMR	2010–2011
Fischer Racing (as Young Driver AMR)	2010–2011

THE RACING

A full account of every race in which the DBR9 participated is beyond the scope of this book, but what follows is an outline of the major events in the type's racing career.

The 2005 Season

The DBR9 made its racing debut in the 2005 season in the colours of Aston Martin Racing (GB). The cars were entered for both US and European events in order to obtain maximum media coverage, and they did not disappoint. The very first event for DBR9/1 was the Sebring 12 Hours in the Le Mans Series held in the USA, where the car achieved a win in the GT1 category.

Two cars were entered for the Le Mans 24 Hours, but fuel problems held the leading DBR9/1 back and it finished in third place in the GT1 category behind Corvette Racing, and ninth in the overall classification. This car ran as number 59 and was driven by David Brabham, Stéphane Sarrazin, and Darren Turner. The second car ran as number 58 and did not finish the event; its crew was Peter Kox, Pedro Lamy and Tomas Enge, all of whom would be chosen for many further drives in DBR9s.

The 2006 Season

The number of teams using the DBR9 proliferated this year, as early cars were rolled out for the works-affiliated teams of BMS and Larbre, and the first customer teams were also able to field cars.

In the FIA GT Championship, the DBR9s started the season as favourites, but unfortunately did not live up to expectations, with just two victories at Mugello and Dubai. At the Spa 24 Hours in July, Phoenix Racing came a close second to the winning Maserati, and the BMS team DBR9 finished in fourth place.

Works-supported Larbre Compétition campaigned the DBR9 fiercely in the Le Mans Endurance series and took the Team Championship, with victories in the 1,000 Kilometre races in Istanbul and at the Nürburgring, a second place at Jarama, and a fifth place at Donington.

The two-car entry for the Le Mans 24 Hours this year wore racing numbers 007 (in honour of the James Bond association) and 009 (in honour of the DBR9 itself). Sadly, the best they could achieve was second in the GT1 class and sixth overall with car number 007, driven by Darren Turner, Tomas Enge and Andrea Piccini. Car number 009 was certainly not disgraced, however, and with its drivers Pedro Lamy, Stéphane Sarrazin and Stéphane Ortelli, it came fifth in the GT1 class and tenth overall.

Over in the USA, Aston Martin Racing regularly challenged the eventual winners Corvette Racing for top positions in the American Le Mans Series, and achieved victories at Lime Rock, Miller Motorsports Park, Mosport, the Petit Le Mans (held at Road Atlanta) and Laguna Seca. They finished the season second in the manufacturers' category of the GT1 Championship.

The 2007 Season

The 2007 season saw the DBR9's third attempt on the Le Mans 24 Hours, and this time it was rewarded with a win in the GT1 class. This somewhat eclipsed the cars'

The real thing: a 2006 DBRS9 is pictured in the headquarters of Prodrive, at Banbury.

One of the works cars wore race number 007 from 2006, when this picture was taken in the workshops at Prodrive.

Car number 100 of BMS Scuderia Italia was pictured at the Le Mans test day in 2007.

Car number 009 was the Le Mans winner, and was pictured here at a Prodrive open day in 2007 with Johnny Herbert at the wheel.

achievements elsewhere, but for Aston Martin it was a very important victory. Every single DBR9 entered in the event this year finished, which was a testament to the reliability and endurance of the latest race cars. On the back of this success, Aston Martin brought to market a limited-edition version of the road-going DB9 named after the Le Mans event (and there is more about it in Chapter 6).

The winning car at Le Mans wore number 009, and was driven for Aston Martin Racing by David Brabham, Darren Turner and Rickard Rydell. The class win was accompanied by a fifth place overall. Not far behind, finishing third in the GT1 class and seventh overall, was car number 008, run by the Larbre team and driven by Christophe Bouchut, Fabrizio Gollin and Casper Elgaard. Right behind them, taking fourth

Darren Turner piloted the DBR9 for the works team at Le Mans and was one of the crew of the car that won the GT1 category in 2007. He subsequently moved to Fischer Racing.

in class and ninth place overall, was car number 007 of Aston Martin Racing (GB), driven by Johnny Herbert, Peter Kox and Tomas Enge.

The set was completed by the BMS car (number 100) that came sixth in the GT1 class and eleventh overall, in the hands of Fabio Baini, Jamie Davies and Matteo Malucelli. Then the last DBR9 home was car number 006, wearing race number 006. This finished thirteenth in its class and 29th overall, driven by Patrick Bornhauser, Roland Berville and Gregor Fisken.

The 2008 Season

There were changes in the works team representation for the 2008 season. The Larbre and BMS teams no longer fielded DBR9s, but Aston Martin Racing (GB) remained partnered with Prodrive and took on Gulf Oil as its major sponsor. The cars therefore competed in the Gulf Oil colours of orange and eggshell blue. Alain Dujean, a vice president of Gulf Oil, expressed his hopes for 'a long and fruitful partnership', and Prodrive's David Richards, who was by this stage also Chairman of Aston Martin itself, said of the DBR9's attempt on Le Mans this year:

> *Endurance racing is engrained in the heritage of both Gulf and Aston Martin and we have also both been intrinsically linked through Le Mans for many decades. It was perhaps destined that, in the year we defend our GT1 title and Gulf celebrates the 40th anniversary of its win [with a Ford GT40 in 1968], we would finally race together at La Sarthe.*

The two AMR (GB) cars once again wore the race numbers 007 and 009, and car 009, driven by David Brabham, Antonio Garcia and Darren Turner, did all that was expected of it. Its class win repeated the 2007 victory, and was accompanied by a thirteenth place overall. Fourth in class and in sixteenth place overall was the second car, number 007 driven by Heinz-Harald Frentzen, Andrea Piccini and Karl Wendlinger.

The 2009 Season

Aston Martin and Prodrive considered that they had achieved all they could with the DBR9, and in January 2009 announced that they would focus on a works entry at

For the 2008 season, the cars wore the striking Gulf Oil livery of orange and eggshell blue.

Le Mans consisting of Lola-Aston Martin B09/60 cars with their V12 engine. These would run in the LMP (Le Mans Prototype) category.

Nevertheless, the DBR9's racing career was very far from over. During the 2009 season, a Le Mans-specification car raced in the Japanese Super GT series.

The 2010 Season

For the 2010 season, the FIA announced a two-year homologation waiver that allowed Aston Martin and others to enter the GT1 World Championship. As 2009 drew to a close, Aston Martin therefore announced a new partnership with Fischer Racing at Paderborn in Germany, which would campaign the DBR9 in the new series. Aston Martin works drivers Darren Turner, Tomas Enge and Stefan Mücke would all join the new team, and Fischer Racing would provide their existing driver, Christoffer Nygaard.

For the 2010 season, the team raced two new cars under the name of Young Driver AMR, which reflected its association with the Young Driver programme. The racing schedule included an entry into the Le Mans 24 Hours, where Enge, Nygaard and Peter Kox took car number 52 to third place in its class and 22nd in the overall classification.

The 2011 Season

A second team was selected to run DBR9s in the 2011 season of the FIA GT1 World Championship alongside Young Driver AMR. This was Hexis Racing, an established team with headquarters at Lédenon in France. Hexis had been racing three DBRS9 models in the GT3 class since 2007, and for 2011 switched to the DBR9 in the top GT category.

After a handful of early victories, Hexis went through a bad patch in mid-season. However, consistent points finishes for both its cars and a podium place at the San Luis round gave Hexis a narrow victory in the Team Championship. Drivers Civio Piccione and Stef Dusseldorp in car number 3 also came third in the Drivers' Championship. However, the DBR9's two-year homologation waiver ran out at the end of the 2011 season, and the cars were no longer eligible to compete in later GT1 World Championship seasons.

The racing Astons were campaigned by the Hexis team from 2010 onwards. This picture was taken at Silverstone in 2011.

THE DBRS9

The cost of running a car such as the DBR9 in a full season's race series is huge, and way beyond the resources of many smaller teams. Yet restricting a race car to only a small number of teams reduces its publicity value for the marque behind it, and so in order to get maximum exposure for their venture into racing with the DB9, Aston Martin resolved to offer a less expensive customer car alongside the DBR9. Benefiting from much of the engineering that went into the DBR9 itself, the DBRS9 sister car was announced in late 2005.

The DBRS9 was deliberately pitched at the FIA GT3 class, and was also eligible for some national and international GT series, including the British GT Championship. The base price at its launch was around £175,000 before taxes and without any additions to the core specification. Much of the car was the same as the DBR9, with the same uprated suspension, stiffer racing springs and lower ride height. The body structure again depended on carbon-fibre panels instead of the road car's aluminium ones, with polycarbonate side and rear windows, while the deliberately Spartan cabin was protected by a full race-specification roll cage.

However, there were two major differences between the DBRS9 and its DBR9 sibling. The first lay in its weight, which was some 60kg (132lb) greater, at 1,230kg (2,712lb) – and yet still considerably lower than that of the DB9 road car at 1,710kg (3,770lb). The second important difference lay in its engine, which was not as powerful as the full race-spec type. Nevertheless, with 550bhp (558PS) and 457lb ft (620Nm) of torque in ex-factory tune, it was still considerably more powerful than the road car version, which in 2005 had 450bhp and 420lb ft of torque. All cars came with a six-speed close-ratio manual gearbox, either a conventional type or a sequential type. The 0–60mph standing-start time of a DBRS9 was claimed to be the same 3.4sec as the DBR9, while the top speed was 195mph (314km/h).

Teams from several countries raced the DBRS9. In Britain, the main effort came from Barwell Motorsport. Italian input was initially from BMS Scuderia Italia, but after the 2007 season the partnership with Aston Martin was ended and the cars were raced under the name of Brixia Racing. From France came Hexis Racing, Belgium had Racing for Belgium, and Germany had Phoenix Racing. There were also two teams in Australia: ABCOR and VIP Petfoods.

The heyday of the DBRS9's racing career was between 2006 and 2009, although the cars continued to race in lower-level events long after that, and continued to attract the attention for which they had been designed. From 2011, a version of the V12 Vantage replaced them as the Aston Martin GT3 car.

THE CARS

There was one prototype car, which was finished in dark metallic grey and was seen in early publicity pictures. This was followed by eighteen race cars, making a grand total of just nineteen DBR9s. The build numbers suggest that ten were intended for Aston Martin Racing and its affiliated teams, and nine for customer teams. In practice, one of the 'customer' cars was not built, and two of the 'AMR' cars were sold to customer teams. This table contains brief notes about each one; fuller details can be found on the web site www.racingsportscars.com.

DBR9/1

This was raced by Aston Martin Racing at Le Mans in 2005, when it finished third in its class. At the Sebring 12hrs event, it came fourth overall and won the GT1 class.

For the 2006 season, the car passed to Larbre, who raced it in the Le Mans series. In 2007, the same team raced it in the FFSA GT Championship and at the Le Mans 24 Hours.

For the 2010 season, the car was run by the Hexis AMR team and competed in FIA GT1 World Championship events. Hexis again campaigned this car in the 2011 FIA GT1 World Championship, and finished the season with the team prize.

DBR9/2

Like DBR9/1, this car initially raced for Aston Martin Racing in the 2005 season. Its best result was second place overall in the Silverstone Tourist Trophy in May. At Le Mans in June it did not finish because of fuel problems, which was disappointing after it had won the GT1 category in the Le Mans Test earlier in the month.

DBR9/2 was transferred to the Larbre team for the 2007 season, but achieved no victories or podium finishes. It then went to the Hexis team. In 2010 it came second in the Silverstone Tourist Trophy race in May, and then won the San Luis event in December. The following year was also successful, with a second place at Zolder in April and a win in the ADFAC Masters event at the Sachsenring in May.

DBR9/3

DBR9/3 raced for Aston Martin Racing at the Le Mans 24 Hours in 2006, and in that year it also took two wins in the American Le Mans series. In the 2007 season it was raced by the Larbre team, including at the Le Mans 24 Hours.

DBR9/4

DBR9/4 was the first car to go to a customer team, and in 2006 it was campaigned by Team Modena in the Le Mans Series, achieving a single class win. It then passed to Strakka Racing, who entered it in the 2008 Le Mans 24 Hours event under the banner of the Vitaphone Racing Team.

DBR9/5

DBR9/5 was another customer car, which was campaigned by Bell Motorsports in the 2008 Le Mans Series. It ran in six races and achieved four podium places, but no class wins.

DBR9/6

The sixth DBR9 went to the works-supported BMS team, who raced it in the 2006 and 2007 FIA GT Championships. Its best result in 2006 was a fourth place at the Spa Proxius 24 that was held in July, but the 2007 season's results were fairly lacklustre after a fifth place at Monza in February. The car was later used by the Young Driver AMR team at some events in 2011.

DBR9/7

Chassis number 7 went to the BMS team for 2006 and raced in the full season of the FIA GT Championship. It achieved some fourth and fifth places, but there were no podium places or class wins.

DBR9/8

Aston Martin Racing (GB) ran DBR9/8 in the American Le Mans Series during the 2006 season. The car achieved class wins at Lime Rock in July, at the Mospor Grand Prix in September, and again at Laguna Seca in October, but its best overall placing was fourth at the Lime Rock event.

For the 2007 season, the car ran in the FIA GT Championship for the BMS team, its best result being a third place at the Adria event in September. Back with Aston Martin Racing (GB) for the 2008 season, it won the GT1 class at the Le Mans Test Day and also at the Le Mans 24 Hours event itself, although it was placed only thirteenth overall in the latter event.

DBR9/9

DBR9/9 was run by the BMS team in the 2006 FIA GT Championship, when it achieved third places at Silverstone in May, and Brno in May, and at the Hungaroring in October. It did not finish at the Le Mans 24 Hours.

continued

continued

Entered in the same championship for the 2007 season, it finished third at Oschersleben in July but was then written off in a major accident at the Spa 24 Hours later that month.

DBR9/10

The tenth DBR9 race car was new for the 2007 season and ran only at the Le Mans 24 Hours in June (in addition to the Le Mans Test earlier in the month). In that event it ran as car number 009 and won the GT1 class, while finishing in fifth place overall.

DBR9/101

DBR9/101, a 2005 car, was initially prepared by Cirtek Motorsport, who first ran it in the Le Mans Series with the livery of Russian Age Racing. In its second race, at the Nürburging in September, the car finished first in the GT1 class and came ninth overall. Cirtek then switched to the FIA GT Championship, and the car finished first in Bahrain in November.

Cirtek remained the owners of the car for the 2006 season, but this time it raced in the colours of Modena Racing. Its best result was a class win and fourth overall at Donington Park. For the 2007 season, the car ran in the European Le Mans Series but in March was also taken to the USA, where it came third in class at the Sebring 12 Hours race.

The car's final racing season was 2008, when it ran in four races of the Le Mans Series. It achieved three first places and a third, missing out on championship victory by just one point.

DBR9/101 was subsequently returned to its 2006 specification and has been displayed at several venues and events.

DBR9/102

Wealthy Brazilian businessman Alcides Diniz bought the second customer example of the DBR9 for his Capuava Racing Team. It was specified with a 75bhp power increase over the 2005 figure, a paddle-shift gearchange, and a larger front splitter and rear wing.

The car was entered for the Mil Milhas Brasileiras in January 2006 but developed engine problems in practice and did not compete in the race. Owner Alcides Diniz died later that year and the car was sold on. It still races today in the Global and Masters Endurance Legends series.

DBR9/103

The third customer DBR9 was one of two sold to the Austrian RaceAlliance team for FIA GT Championship events. It first appeared at the Paul Ricard Test Days in March 2006, where it claimed second place, but early races were unproductive. A second place at Dijon and a win at Mugello in September showed promise, but the rest of the season was disappointing.

From March 2007, RaceAlliance became JetAlliance, and DBR9/103 racked up an impressive three wins, at Monza in June, Adria in September, and Zolder in October. The 2008 season was less successful, its highlight being a second place at Oschersleben in July; the car ran its last races in 2009, the final one being the Le Mans 24 Hours, where its place was disappointing.

DBR9/104

Phoenix Racing bought DBR9/104 and campaigned it determinedly in the 2006 FIA GT Championship. They were rewarded with two third places (at Oschersleben in July and Dijon in September), two second places (Brno in May and Spa in July), and a win at Dubai in November.

Despite this very promising record, the DBR9 was sidelined for 2007 after appearing at Monza in February for the FIA GT tests. It was given a last outing at Zolder in October but did not finish the race. Phoenix Racing moved on to the less expensive Corvette GT1 for 2008, and DBR9/104 was sold to Team Nova in Japan, who campaigned it in national events during 2009. The car also became the subject of a Scalextric model.

DBR9/105

DBR9/105 was the second car to go to JetAlliance, who were newly renamed from RaceAlliance in 2007. It first appeared in FIA GT Championship events in the 2007 season, but its best result was a seventh place at Monza in June. The 2008 season was much more successful, and DBR9/105 returned one third place (at Zolder in October) and no fewer than three wins (at Silverstone in April, Oschersleben in July, and Brno in September).

DBR9/106

DBR9/106 went initially to Barwell Motorsport for the FIA GT Championship, and appeared in their colours at Zhuhai in March and Silverstone in May. However, over the summer the car changed hands, and in October made its first appearance for Gigawave Motorsport. This was probably always intended as no more than a first trial, and Gigawave campaigned the car with some energy during the 2008 GT Championship.

continued

continued

Car number 106 finished the season with a creditable haul of four third places (Nogaro and Silverstone in April, Monza in May, and Spa in August), plus one second place at Monza in March.

Gigawave entered the car for the Le Mans 24 Hours in 2009, but changed their allegiance to the Nissan GT-R GT1 during the season and withdrew the DBR9. The car's last race for the Gigawave team was at Silverstone in September, when it won the GT1 class but was placed nineteenth overall.

DBR9/107 and DBR9/108

There is some confusion about these cars. One story is that they were not built but were replaced as customer cars by DBR9/4 and DBR9/5, which then carried the numbers of the unbuilt cars.

However, DBR9/108 seems to have been used by Young Driver AMR. It was displayed at Brno in May 2010 and was probably raced several times in the 2010 season alongside DBR9/109, which also belonged to the team.

DBR9/109

DBR9/109 was built for the 2010 FIA GT1 World Championship season and was raced by Young Driver AMR. Its first appearance was at the FIA GT Paul Ricard test day in February, and in March it won the GT1 category at the Le Mans Series test day. It was also entered for the Spa 1000km, but was severely damaged in an accident during that event.

The 2006 Season

In their first season on the tracks, DBRS9s were campaigned in the GT3 category of the FIA European Championship, the FIA GT Championship and the British GT Championship.

Barwell Motorsport entered the European Championship and the British GT Championship. Their three cars appeared in four rounds of the latter, and the team finished the season with second place in the Team Championship, while driver Leo Machitski claimed the Drivers' Championship title.

BMS won at Oschersleben in the European Championship, but did not finish at the Spa 24 Hours event. In the GT Championship they took two wins, at the Hungaroring and in Dubai.

The 2007 Season

The 2007 season saw the cars running in the same three race series as in 2006, plus the ADAC GT Masters and the Australian GT Championship.

In the British GT Championship, Barwell Motorsport took the team title, while drivers Jonathan Cocker and (Lord) Paul Drayson came second in the Drivers' Championship. A new DBRS9 team this year was Cadena Motorsport. In the FIA Championship, meanwhile, BMS remained a participant, along with Hexis Racing and its associate team, Racing for Belgium. BMS finished second in the Team Championship. Racing for Belgium also competed in the ADAC GT Masters, where Phoenix Racing also campaigned DBRS9 cars. Aston Martin Austria teamed up with Phoenix Racing to enter a car with race number 007 in the Nürburgring 24 Hours race; the car led the race in the early stages but succumbed to engine failure on the second day.

Meanwhile Preston General Engineering (a division of the ABCOR Group) raced a DBRS9 in a number of rounds of the 2007 Australian GT Championship.

The 2008 Season

In the 2008 season, the DBRS9s continued to race in the FIA Championship, the ADAC GT Masters, the British GT Championship and the Australian series.

In the British series, 22GT Racing and Cadena Motorsport took over the cars from Barwell racing, but their season was not very successful. In Australia, the ABCOR team continued their campaign, and later in the season were joined by DBRS9s from Team Aston Martin and VIP Petfoods Racing.

Brixia Racing took over the BMS cars in the FIA Championship for 2008. Meanwhile, Hexis Racing remained in contention and in this year finished second in both the Drivers' and the Team Championships. Hexis this year moved their DBRS9s from French FFSA GT events to the German ADAC GT Masters series, where their DBRS9s earned them third place in the Team Championship.

The 2009 Season

2009 was the final major season for the DBRS9s, although examples continued to race for many years afterwards in lower-level events.

In the DBRS9, the V12 engine had a lower state of tune than the version in the DBR9 but was still formidably powerful. This underbonnet shot shows the Aston Martin Racing branding, and the identity of the engine itself – DBRS 1001, as seen on the left-hand cam cover.

The Young Driver AMR car driven by Turner and Enge was pictured at Silverstone in 2010.

This DBRS9 was pictured at an event in Paris during the Blancpain Endurance Series in March 2011.

A pair of DBR9s in action on the track at the Sachsenring in Germany in 2011.

Under the bonnet of DBRS9 number 23, with engine number 1027; once again, the identity is shown on a small plate on the cam cover nearer the camera. The picture dates from 2011.

At home in Britain, Barwell Motorsport joined forces with Beechdean Motorsport to campaign a joint Barwell-Beechdeam DBRS9 in British GT events. 22GT Racing also continued competing in the British GT series with their DBRS9. Barwell Motorsport also secured sponsorship from Aston Martin Brussels and entered two DBRS9s in the Belgian GT Championship, but without great success.

In Australia, VIP Petfoods Racing continued to run a DBRS9 in Australian GT races, while in Europe both Brixia Racing and Hexis Racing stayed with the Aston Martin DBRS9 in the FIA Championship. The Hexis effort was in fact split between GT3 and GT2 events (with an Aston Martin Vantage supported by Aston Martin Racing), but three wins in the GT3 category led to the Team Championship title and a second place in the Drivers' Championship.

Still racing in 2018, this is DBRS9 number 23 at the 1000 Tours du Castellet held on the Circuit Paul Ricard in south-eastern France.

CHAPTER 8

THE MID-PERIOD DB9, 2009–2012

Six years on from its launch at Frankfurt in 2003, Aston Martin considered that the DB9 was due for some more major revisions in order to retain its appeal and remain fresh. No doubt there was some encouragement from Ford in Detroit, too, as that company had long mastered the art of regular and usually well-judged model updates. In practice, there would be regular annual updates for the DB9 over the next few years, including the release of some special editions, which added even more exclusivity to the ownership of one of these cars.

THE 2009 MODELS

The refreshed 2009 models were formally announced in July 2008, although some examples had been completed before then and *Car* magazine was able to drive one and report on it for its issue dated 7 May. The headline changes were a revised V12 engine with 470bhp, and a new control system for the ZF automatic gearbox, and these were supplemented by suspension improvements and an interior redesign. Nevertheless, there were no major changes to the

Displaying one of Aston Martin's regular number-plates, a 2009 DB9 Coupé shows the latest specification with five-bar grille.

car's exterior appearance. The easiest recognition point was the new wheels, with a choice that now included some 20in options, although a closer examination would reveal a new five-bar anodised grille, and new door mirrors with taller bodies but thinner supporting arms, like the ones that had been introduced on the DBS.

Car magazine found plenty of detail to criticise, but concluded that 'These latest tweaks provide real lustre to the DB9, broadening its appeal as a GT and adding bite to its ultimate performance. An already desirable car just got that bit more desirable…' They added that their test car was 'a showcase for the constant development that Aston Martin has been carrying out on the DB9 over the past years: both subtle and more fundamental engineering changes that don't feature on any press material.'

The 2009-model DB9 coupé and Volante both had the revised engine, which was known as the AM09 type (the link between the 2009 model-year and the 09 designation should be obvious). This delivered 20bhp more than the earlier AM04 type, together with an extra 23lb ft of torque. Both peak figures were achieved at the same engine revolutions as before. These increases in output were achieved primarily by redesigned cylinder heads and a raised compression ratio. There certainly had been no lack of attention to detail, and an additional change had been to a deeper sump, which Aston Martin claimed reduced drag on the crankshaft. Models with the new 470bhp engine were capable of 306km/h (190mph), a 7km/h (4mph) increase on their predecessors.

Allied to these engine changes was a new hydraulic control unit with associated software for the ZF automatic gearbox. Known as Touchtronic 2, this offered faster gear shifts, mainly to the benefit of acceleration – although *Car* magazine noticed other improvements as well. 'The shifts are certainly faster and smoother when you're going flat out,' they reported, 'plus there's noticeably less time taken to swop cogs at walking pace – when you're executing a three-point turn for example.' In tandem with the extra torque of the 2009-specification engine, this did improve the 0–60mph acceleration time by 0.1sec to 4.6sec – a figure that seems a little underwhelming for all the effort that had been made. There were, of course, further gains at higher speeds.

Aston Martin had also taken note of earlier criticisms of the DB9's suspension, and had put some effort into making improvements. A combination of carefully tuned bushes and Bilstein dampers had brought about a very worthwhile improvement, and *Car* magazine thought that the new suspension 'tackles all manner of roads with a genuine pliancy that never degenerates into a wallow.' They went on to say that, 'along with greatly reduced road and wind noise, this is now a comfortable car for

A 2009 Volante displays the operation of its powered roof, which was stowed in a compartment ahead of the boot when not in use.

Clear lenses for the tail lights were part of the 2009 specification. They appeared red when the light behind was lit.

For 2009, this crystal key fob replaced the earlier starter button. It had been pioneered on the new DBS flagship of the range.

long distances – much more so than the over-firm original – and yet it's still engrossing on the right road thanks to light but accurate steering and a chassis always ready to be steered from your right boot.'

Despite its sweeping good looks, the centre stack of instruments and controls had never been wholly convincing, and Aston Martin now addressed this on the 2009 model-year cars by importing the version of the design introduced for the flagship DBS model that had replaced the Vanquish S in 2008. Unfortunately this was not quite the success that the company had hoped for: 'The plastics simply feel too cheap,' said *Car* magazine, adding that 'they are easily marked, and the morass of buttons is initially unfathomable and then pedantic in operation.' Retaining the Volvo-sourced navigation system was also 'a shame'.

Another feature pioneered on the DBS also showed up on the 2009-model DB9, and that was a crystal key fob that had to be inserted into the facia to start the car. It replaced the earlier glass starter button whose illumination changed from blue to red when the engine was started. It was an attractive and tactile thing, but for reasons best known to themselves, Aston Martin had chosen to call it an Emotion Control Unit. That description may have appealed to some customers – and the Aston Martin marketing team knew their customers better than anybody – but the whole concept did not appeal to *Car* magazine. The writers also seized their opportunity to take a swipe at 'the ludicrously small rear-seat compartment', which took up space that 'would be more useful as a dedicated luggage area.' Yet

THE BANG & OLUFSEN ICE SYSTEM

The Bang & Olufsen sound system for the Aston Martin DB9 was announced in a press release dated 2 April 2009 and became available as an option on the 2010 models. It could be fitted in place of the standard Linn ICE system.

The system was called the BeoSound DB9, and continued the association between the two brands that had begun with a system for the Aston Martin DBS in 2008. The new system was developed specifically for the DB9 to provide a perfect match both physically and acoustically, and a special version had been developed for the DB9 Volante to suit that model's individual characteristics, whether open or closed.

Switching on the system caused a pair of tweeters to emerge silently from either side of the dashboard. These were equipped with B&O's patented Acoustic Lens Technology, and their placement gave listeners in each of the car's seats an improved sense of space, staging and realism. Eleven more speakers were positioned around the car, including three more tweeters and three woofers, the latter including a powerful 200mm sub-woofer mounted below the rear bench seat. All those visible were faced with aluminium grilles that were carefully matched to the forms and textures of the interior trim.

The system also used a DSP (digital signal processing) unit, which adapted automatically to changing road and noise conditions, reducing the need to alter the volume or balance characteristics while on the move.

on the positive side they said that 'the interior is inspired at times, with rich leathers creating an aura beyond any German rival.'

THE 2010 MODELS

The most important change to the DB9 for the 2010 season was the addition of the ADS – adaptive damper system – as part of a new Premium Sports Pack option. A version of the system had already been available on the DBS model, but for the DB9 it was re-tuned to suit the less expensive car's softer grand touring characteristics.

The system was arranged to give five different damper settings, which were controlled electronically from a central adaptive damping ECU. This in turn depended on signals from sensors around the car that picked up the current dynamic conditions and interpreted the driver's demands. The ECU adjusted the dampers – each one independently – to maximise tyre contact with the road surface, and was capable of reacting to changes within a fraction of a second.

The driver had a degree of direct control from a button (with a damper icon) on the centre console, which would make the change from the default Normal setting to a Sport setting. In practice, the system could use all five settings when in Normal mode if the conditions warranted it; it simply favoured the firmer settings in Sport mode. That control button on the centre console was the only evidence inside the car that ADS was fitted, but Aston Martin knew that many customers would want more tangible evidence to give them bragging rights, and so ADS came with distinctive five-spoke alloy wheels as well.

Also introduced during the lifetime of the 2010 models, although not actually previewed until the Geneva Show in March 2010, was a new bespoke finishing service known as Works Tailored. Several other premium car brands offered such a service, and it was important for Aston Martin to keep up with its rivals. In the words of Kingsley Riding-Felce, the company's Director of Works Service & Parts Operations, 'So many customers have been expressing an interest in us preparing bespoke features for their cars that we realised the only option was to expand this area of the business and make it open to all.'

Works Tailored was set up to make mostly cosmetic changes to the standard specification of all Aston Martin models, and as examples the company cited custom colour combinations, fitting a mini fridge, and embroidering the owner's initials into the headrests and the carpets. The plan was also to offer wheels that would refresh the appearance of existing cars, and at this stage Aston Martin had a total of thirteen options (not all of which were for the DB9), including 20in sizes, and finishes that ranged from flat graphite through silver to diamond-turned.

The physical demonstration of the new service at Geneva consisted of two specially prepared cars, one of them a Rapide model and the other a DB9. The DB9 had been painted in pearlescent Blue Pearl White with contrasting gunmetal exterior metal trim, while its interior was trimmed in Blue Gin leather and featured African Walnut highlights finished in Mink Grey.

THE 2011 MODELS

Aston Martin announced the 2011 models in June 2010 for a start to sales in July, and in line with the company's philosophy of continual improvement, there were multiple incremental changes. As far as the engine was concerned, the change was a 'green' one: without affecting the power and torque outputs, some careful engineering had reduced the CO_2 emissions figures by nearly 50g/km to 345g/km. This change mattered more in some countries where the car was sold than in others, but of course all buyers of a 2011 model could point to its 'green' credentials if they wished.

There were some visual touches, too. Director of Design Marek Reichman was quoted as saying that: 'We are continuing the elegant feel of the DB9: there's a new front bumper, new side skirts, new colours.... These are mild changes – we've made 12,000 DB9s since launch and don't feel the need to start afresh.' But, he added, 'There are also plenty of under-the-skin changes.'

The new side skirts were reshaped and brought a more exaggerated hockey-stick highlight to the flanks, which was more visible on the lighter-coloured cars. There were small changes to the rear bumper, the tail lights now had the clear lenses first seen on the 2008 Le Mans edition, while the front grille now sported a two-level design with a hexagonal mesh for the lower section. Then there were some new wheel designs as well, although a twenty-spoke diamond-turned design was standard. These accompanied what was perhaps the most important change of all: the Adaptive Damping System first seen on the DBS now became standard equipment, and the Premium Sports Pack was therefore withdrawn as redundant.

Car magazine's Tim Pollard drove back to the UK from Le Mans in an early example, after being embedded in the Aston Martin Racing pit team during the annual 24 Hours event. He reported on the DB9 drive for the magazine's online presence on 17 June 2010, and felt that Aston's philosophy of continual improvement had resulted in a car that was vastly better than the DB9 that had been launched in 2003: 'It's clear that great strides have been made to iron out those early faults,' he wrote. 'Perhaps chief exec Ulrich Bez has finally imbued some Germanic values on the production line, for this DB9 feels top drawer.'

He thought that the coupé:

> *...looks every inch the £122,445 sports car from every angle. I especially love the coke-bottle swell to the hips that lends the DB9 a sprung, muscular feel. But I find the steering wheel quite ugly, its airbag-shaped centre boss being too chunky for what is an elegant, classy cabin. And – we've been saying it for years and it's becoming truer by the year – that the Volvo pop-up sat-nav is a disgrace; rotating screens are passé in 2010, while the graphics, speed of operation and user interface are way off the pace.*

This car had the Touchtronic 2 automatic gearbox, like more than 95 per cent of DB9s then being ordered:

> *There's still no gearlever, and it's all the better for it in here. Push the D button high on the dash and the DB9 creeps forwards just like a proper slusher. This gearbox suits the DB9's temperament – you can pootle around town or power down a back road and it always seems to be in the right gear.*
>
> *A Sport button on the dash programmes the ECU to hang on to gears for longer, but we found the standard setting to be fine most of the time. You'll love the paddles, though, which let you nudge into manual mode whenever the mood takes you. And this one really does over-ride the computer – you're in charge, and it won't change up for you, though it will downshift if you're about to stall.*

Pollard noted that the engine had to be revved to get the best performance from the DB9, whose maximum torque was generated at a high 5,000rpm. But he found the car 'well judged, with clout when you need it and whispery quietness when you're wafting.' Only the brakes came in for criticism, as they were difficult to modulate at low speeds and tended to grab as the car came to rest.

The 2011 Special Editions

Highlight of the 2011 model-year was the announcement on 22 December 2010 of not one, but three special editions of the DB9. These were called the Carbon Black, the Morning Frost, and the Quantum Silver, and in all cases were available either as a coupé or a Volante convertible. All of them came with the standard 470bhp 6.0-litre V12 engine, and with the six-speed Touchtronic 2 automatic gearbox. However, each one had its own individual cosmetic features. Aston Martin has never released details of production totals for these cars, which were made available globally, but it is reasonable to assume that numbers were limited at the very least to no more than one car for each dealer.

The DB9 Carbon Black was deliberately dressed to look menacing, and to reinforce that image it came with a distinctively tuned exhaust system. It had the Carbon Black paint that its name suggested, and this was matched by black grilles, graphite tailpipes and diamond-turned 19in ten-spoke alloy wheels with gloss black highlights. The interior was trimmed in Obsidian Black, with silver stitching for the leather and polished glass for the switch gear. The wearing surfaces of the seats were upholstered with perforated leather, there was highly polished Piano Black on the centre console and the door handles, and the headlining was made of semi-aniline leather. The Carbon Black name was also carried on laser-etched sill plates that also carried the Aston Martin winged logo.

In stark contrast to the Carbon Black edition, the DB9 Morning Frost had a bright pearlescent white paint finish. Exterior detailing was in silver, with Magnum Silver grilles and silver brake callipers visible through the diamond-turned, 19in, ten-spoke wheels with silver highlights.

This was a deliberately less aggressive special edition, and had a standard exhaust system rather than the tuned one of the Carbon Black. The interior in these models was trimmed with metallic bronze leather, again with perforated wearing surfaces on the seats and Piano Black on the centre console and door handles. The headlining was trimmed in matching metallic bronze leather. In this case, the laser-etched sill plates of course carried the Morning Frost name alongside the winged Aston Martin logo.

As for the Quantum Silver models, these were finished in the dark metallic silver used on the Aston Martin DBS

Everything in black and white: this publicity picture from 2011 promoted the Carbon Black Coupé and the Morning Frost Volante – although both models were available in both colours.

The 2011 Carbon Black edition certainly lived up to its name visually. Even the diamond-turned spokes of the alloy wheels had black highlights.

in the 2008 James Bond 007 film *Quantum of Solace*. Like the Carbon Black edition, they had a tuned sports exhaust system, and they had the same 19in, ten-spoke, diamond-turned wheels with gloss black highlights. Also like the Carbon Black, they came with black grilles and graphite tail pipes. The interior was again like that of the Carbon Black, with black leather featuring perforated seat-wearing surfaces, Piano Black highlights and polished glass switchgear. The laser-etched sill plates of course bore the Quantum Silver name.

The all-black theme continued for the interior of the Carbon Black edition: the upholstery was Obsidian Black and the trim sections were Piano Black.

A black headlining of semi-aniline leather completed the Carbon Black edition's interior picture.

With all that black inside and out, the label on the sill plate was perhaps superfluous!

An example of the Morning Frost Volante was displayed at the Geneva Show in 2011.

Branded brake callipers were visible through the delicate ten-spoke wheels of the Morning Frost edition.

This view of the Morning Frost Volante makes clear that it had the '+2' option of the fully upholstered rear seats.

WHAT THE PRESS THOUGHT

In its early days the DB9 had produced some quite violently contrasting reactions from the press, and many of these are quoted in earlier chapters of this book. Some testers absolutely loved it, but there were many who were more lukewarm in their reactions, tending to focus on what they saw as faults that they expected Aston Martin to sort out.

Over the years the company had done just that, and although the DB9 was still not entirely flawless, it was by this stage more generally accepted as a superb machine. Typical of these later reactions were the comments made by *Car* magazine in some online comments dated 18 May 2011:

> *Since its 2003 launch, the DB9 Coupé has matured into something very, very desirable. It's as sorted now as it was a work-in-progress in the early days. It's smooth and refined but can play the stonking supercar with surprising enthusiasm, and with a manual 'box it's an absolute riot. As for the less desirable characteristics, there's still the odd rumble through the steering column, still the odd shake from the structure, but it's a gentle trait rather than an obvious fault.*

It seemed as if the DB9 had at last become the car that Aston Martin had always intended – but of course, further development was in hand.

ENTER THE VIRAGE

At this point in the story it is important to take a look at what else Aston Martin had been doing since the DB9's release in 2003. From 2005 they had expanded the range with a less expensive model called the V8 Vantage that was intended as a Porsche 911 competitor and could be had as either a coupé or, from 2007, a roadster. From 2007, the 510bhp DBS replaced the Vanquish as the flagship model, initially only as a coupé, but from 2009 also as a Volante.

Next, in 2009, came the V12 Vantage, essentially the existing Vantage model but with the V12 engine squeezed under its bonnet in place of the Jaguar-derived V8. That same year, the range was expanded to include a four-door saloon, still based on the VH platform and featuring the V12 engine, with the name of Rapide. From 2010, Aston Martin offered a hypercar rival to the Bugatti Veyron and Pagani Zonda in the form of the limited-volume One-77, with a 750bhp version of the V12 engine in a hand-built, carbon-fibre body

The Virage was a 'gentleman's GT' priced between the DB9 and the flagship DBS. This was the eye-catching coupé model that announced its arrival at the 2011 Geneva Show. MAGIC CAR PICS

The differences between the Virage and the 2011 DB9 were not immediately apparent from the rear, the rear diffuser being a subtle change.

The interior arrangement of the Virage was also very familiar. This was the Geneva Show car.

and a top speed in excess of 355km/h (220mph). (For the sake of completeness, we should also record that 2010 also saw the introduction of the Cygnet, a city car based on the Toyota IQ that Ulrich Bez suggested might complement one of Aston Martin's more traditional cars. Only a few hundred buyers were convinced.)

All this left the company with a far broader range than it had ever had before, and it was clear that Aston Martin saw this as a time of experimentation, a time when this variety of new models explored where the brand might go in the future. And as part of that exploration, the company decided to produce a car that would sit between the DB9 and the DBS.

In the meantime, Aston Martin had continued to refine and develop the VH platform that had made its debut in the DB9. Although that model retained what was essentially a first-generation version of the platform, the 2009 season had brought a number of changes. They were not the first, of course. As early as 2005 the Generation II platform had appeared for the Vantage models, and it had also been central to the new DBS two years later. By 2011, a Generation III version was ready, and this would be the one chosen for the car intended to sit between the DB9 and the DBS.

The new model was introduced at the Geneva Show in March 2011 and took the name of Aston Martin Virage. The name itself was not new: there had been a Virage with the old Aston Martin V8 engine between 1989 and 2000, and this had had the distinction of being the first new Aston Martin to be launched under Ford ownership (although its development had obviously preceded that point). Aston Martin publicity described it as a 'gentleman's GT', and from the start it was made available in both coupé and Volante forms. Pricing set it carefully between the £125,000 DB9 and the £175,000 DBS, at £149,995 for the coupé and an extra £10,000 or so for the Volante – which had an extra sub-frame at the rear to ensure an appropriate degree of body stiffness.

The essential character of the Virage came from a combination of the more supple suspension developed for the four-door Rapide, with a V12 engine uprated to a point midway between its DB9 and DBS specifications. Also central to the concept was that this car should only be available with an automatic gearbox, and it thus became the only Aston Martin of its time not to have a manual gearbox option.

That suspension featured the adaptive dampers from the DBS and the DB9, tuned to the Virage's deliberately

This 2012-model left-hand-drive Virage Volante has the side marker lights required for the US market.

Side marker lights again, this time at the rear of a US-model Virage Volante pictured at an Aston Martin dealership in Connecticut.

more relaxed nature. As usual, there were just two driver-selectable modes, Normal or Sport, but within them the system was able to select any one of five individual settings automatically to suit the road surface and the way the car was being driven. The gearbox was the six-speed ZF 6HP26 with Touchtronic 2 control, and the AM11 version of the V12 engine now delivered 490bhp (497PS). Shorter final-drive gearing added a degree of urge to the in-gear acceleration, too.

All these features were designed to affect the way the car drove, rather than its ultimate performance capability: the top speed of 299km/h (186mph) that Aston Martin claimed was exactly the same as that for the DB9, and the 0–100km/h (62mph) acceleration time was also the same, at 4.6sec. Volante models, incidentally, were limited to a 294km/h (183mph) top speed.

With so much being superficially the same as the DB9, it was important for the Virage to look different, and to this end Marek Reichmann and his team had thoroughly overhauled the appearance. Every single panel except for the roof and boot had been changed, resulting in a tougher and sportier appearance that deliberately fell short of the aggressiveness in the styling of the DBS. The front end had been changed, with a wider grille similar to that on the One-77, and headlights from the Rapide, the rear end now had a subtle rear diffuser, and the sills and side skirts had been emphasised. Wheels with a 20in diameter (as on the DBS) were standard, and the options list included several alternative designs.

However, the interior changes were best described as evolutionary, and at first glance not much had changed from the 2004 DB9. There were metal controls for the electric seats, and the switchgear featured real glass rather than transparent plastic, but these were not readily apparent unless there was a DB9 parked alongside for convenient comparison. All this was something of a disappointment in what was supposed to be a distinctively new car. A further questionable choice was to make the upholstered rear seat standard on Volante models, while the coupés came as standard with a luggage platform at the back and the upholstered seats as an option.

Also on the options list (for both body styles) was a new Bang & Olufsen sound system, and there were a few alternative trim choices. What really did stand out was a new satellite navigation system, which popped up from the top of the dashboard centre stack and was a far more modern proposition than the Volvo-derived system in the less expensive car. It was easier to use, too.

Autocar magazine dated its online review of the Virage to 26 April 2012, and its reactions to the car were not those of unalloyed enthusiasm: 'In most objective ways, this car has moved the game on for Aston, but only marginally. The Virage is far from a revelation. It is, in fact, very much a more broadly talented take on the same recipe.'

The Virage was 'a refined GT car first and a sporting one second', with a personality 'less thrusting' than that of the DBS, and its 'ability to shift between relaxed, easy-going cruiser and a wholly more intense experience is something that differentiates the Virage from its nearest siblings, giving it a broader ability in both disciplines rather than a specialism in either. It's marginal, but still a tangible and defining element of the package.' Very much on the plus side was the car's lazy feel, a result of being 'delightfully over-endowed with urge, even in distinctly non-urgent use.'

Autocar thought that 'the Virage cabin is aesthetically lovely and in keeping with the sumptuous, over-indulgent nature of the car,' but 'there's no doubt it could be better.... improved or not, some of the major elements of the interior are still unforgivably poor for a car of this price.' There was criticism of 'the same central unit in which a glass key is placed to start the car, the same big, square air vents and the same not-quite-good-enough rotating dials and unintuitive wheel-mounted buttons.'

The new Garmin satellite navigation was a major improvement, but the driving position was described as 'hit and miss. Despite the ten-way adjustable seats, it's difficult to get a comfortable position, and the very solid (if nicely supportive) seats are not the best we've seen in top-end GTs.'

The report also complained that the automatic gearbox could be slow to react, and the best acceleration figure that *Autocar* could achieve was 4.9sec for the 0–60mph sprint – which should be compared with the maker's claim of 0–100km/h (62mph) in 4.6sec.

One way or the other, the Virage was not a big success. Aston Martin stopped its production in 2012 after building exactly 1,001 examples in around eighteen months. Of those, 454 were sold in Europe, including 114 for the UK (a total that breaks down further into 22 coupé and 92 Volante models). The official line was that the car was not sufficiently different from the DB9 and the DBS to attract its own group of

There was also a special DB9 Sport edition for some countries, pictured here as a left-hand-drive Volante version for the USA.

The Sport edition had numbered sill plates, as was standard Aston Martin practice at the time.

customers, and a glance at the comparison table below makes clear just how close it was to the DB9 in particular. However, the Virage did have its place in Aston Martin history, as a stage in the development of the DB9, and when it was dropped many of its features became part of the revised DB9 range for 2013.

In the meantime, the DB9 had of course remained on sale for the 2012 model-year, but with no major changes – a policy clearly intended to help increase interest in the new Virage. A 60-strong Sport Edition of the DB9 was announced in May 2012, available as a Coupé or a Volante and with the unique feature of 'pin-stripe' milling on the wheels. There was an extended choice of exterior colours, too. The model was never publicly promoted, but was offered on a personal basis directly to existing Aston Martin customers in North America, Australia and New Zealand.

However, one year of treading water was enough, and for 2013 there would be a number of changes.

A SPECIFICATION COMPARISON

	DB9	Virage	DBS
Power	470bhp/6,000rpm	490bhp/6,500rpm	510bhp/6,500rpm
Torque	443lb ft/5,000rpm	420lb ft/5,750rpm	420lb ft/5,750rpm
Gearbox	Six-speed auto or six-speed manual	Six-speed auto	Six-speed auto or six-speed manual
Final drive	3.46:1		
Max km/h (mph)	299km/h (186mph)	299km/h (186mph)	307km/h (191mph)
0–100km/h	4.6sec	4.6sec	4.2sec
Length	4,710mm (185.4in)	4,719mm (185.78in)	4,721mm (185.86in)
Width	1,880mm (74in) without mirrors	1,905mm (75in) without mirrors	1,905mm (75in) without mirrors
Height	1,270mm (50in)	1,280mm (50.4in)	1,280mm (50.4in)
Wheelbase	2,740mm (107.9in)	2,741mm (107.9in)	2,740mm (107.9in)
Kerb weight	1,760kg (3,880lb)	1,740kg (3,836lb)	1,695kg (3,737lb)
Body styles	Coupé or Volante	Coupé or Volante	Coupé
Price	£125,000 (coupé)	£150,000 (coupé)	£175,000

TECHNICAL SPECIFICATIONS: ASTON MARTIN DB9, 2009–2012

Engine

All-alloy V12 with 4 valves per cylinder.
5935cc (89mm bore x 79.5 stroke).
Four chain-driven overhead camshafts.
Compression ratio 10.8:1.
Visteon engine management.
470bhp at 6,000rpm
443lb ft at 5,000rpm

Gearbox

ZF 6HP26 six-speed automatic with Touchtronic 2 electronic shift-by-wire control system
or
Six-speed Graziano Trasmissioni manual.

Axle ratio

3.15:1

Suspension

Front suspension with double wishbones, incorporating anti-dive geometry, coil springs, anti-roll bar and monotube telescopic dampers; three-stage adaptive dampers from 2010.
Rear suspension with double wishbones with anti-squat and anti-lift geometry, dual-rate coil springs, anti-roll bar and monotube telescopic dampers; three-stage adaptive dampers from 2010.

Steering

Rack-and-pinion steering with standard power assistance.

Brakes

Ventilated discs on all four wheels, with 355mm diameter at the front and 330mm diameter at the rear; carbon ceramic discs optional.
ABS standard, with Brake Assist and Electronic Brakeforce Distribution; Dynamic Stability Control and traction control.

Wheels and tyres

19in (483mm) wheels with 8.5in (216mm) rims at the front and 9.5in (241mm) rims at the rear.
Bridgestone Potenza 235/40ZR19 tyres (front) and 275/35ZR19 tyres (rear)
or (optional)
20in (508mm) wheels with 8.5in (216mm) rims at the front and 11in (279mm) rims at the rear.
Pirelli P-Zero 245/35ZR20 tyres (front) and 295/30ZR20 tyres (rear).

Dimensions

Overall length:	4,710mm (185.4in)
Overall width:	2,017mm (79.4in) over mirrors
Overall height:	1,270mm (50in)
Wheelbase:	2,740mm (107.9in)
Track, front:	1,568mm (61.7in)
Track, rear:	1,562mm (61.5in)

Kerb weight

1,760kg (3,880lb)	Coupé
1,800kg (3,970lb)	Volante

CHAPTER 9

THE LATER DB9, 2013–2016

The VH platform on which all Aston Martin models now depended had been further developed in recent years, but not surprisingly the latest version had appeared first on the most expensive Aston Martin models. As Chapter 8 explains, the Virage had been the first model to receive the Generation III version of it in 2011, and it was also the Virage that provided the inspiration for cosmetic changes on the DB9 that were introduced when the new third-generation structure arrived on the 2013 models. The 2013 models ushered in the second major facelift since the DB9 had entered production some nine years earlier.

Internally the new platform was known as the VH300 type for the DB9 coupé and the VH340 type for the DB9 Volante. None of the platform changes were visible from the outside, however, where the latest facelift adapted design cues from the Virage. The 2013 DB9 was readily recognisable by its different front and rear ends. At the front, the recessed headlight clusters with Bi-Xenon light units and LED daytime running lights were the most obvious change, while a wider front splitter and modified front grille and wing vents completed the picture. The biggest of the rear changes was to the boot lid, where a new spoiler was now an integral part of the design. Also unmissable were the new clear lenses for the LED rear lights.

The visual changes were accompanied by performance improvements, too. The latest AM11 version of the 6.0-litre V12 engine now delivered 510bhp (517PS) with 457lb ft (620Nm) of torque, and shaved a fraction off the 0–60mph acceleration time to give 4.5sec. Maximum speed, however, was now quoted as 295km/h (183mph). Also new for the 2013 cars were the carbon ceramic brakes that had been featured on the Virage and were claimed to give a better response, longer life, and almost complete resistance to fade.

THE CARBON EDITION

The next announcement was another special edition that anticipated the 2015 model-year. Actually announced to the media a few weeks in advance, the Carbon Edition was first shown in public at the Geneva Motor Show that opened on 6 March 2014.

The Carbon Edition followed on from a series that had begun in 2010 with Carbon Black editions of the DBS and the V12 Vantage; there had been a Carbon Black DB9 in 2011, too, matched by a Morning Frost edition in white. This time the matching black and white theme was continued, but the Carbon Black model was matched by a Carbon White version. Both were available as either a coupé or a Volante convertible.

As the name suggested, both variants had some extra carbon-fibre parts, most obviously the side strakes and around the door jambs. There were also black window surrounds to help set off the paintwork, which was either Stratus White or Carbon Black II. Aston Martin has not released figures to show how many of each were built.

THE DB9 GT

Special editions of the DB9 had become something of an annual treat by this stage, but the DB9 GT announced in June 2015 was not a special edition: it was a facelift that added some new features for the DB9's final year. 'Viewed from a business perspective,' said *Top Gear* magazine dated August 2015, 'the GT is a way of garnering a few more sales from an ageing product. But it's hard to view any Aston so coldly.'

THE DB9 SPYDER ZAGATO CENTENNIAL

Aston Martin celebrated its 100th anniversary in 2013, and a special event was held at Kensington Park in London. Among the highlights were two one-off cars created by the Italian coachbuilder Zagato. One was a coupé based on the DBS model, and the other was a convertible based on a DB9. Its full title was the Aston Martin DB9 Spyder Zagato Centennial.

Both cars had been specially commissioned from Zagato by their owners, and Aston Martin staff had not seen the Spyder before it arrived at the centennial celebrations. There had nonetheless been appropriate discussions between Zagato and Aston Martin CEO Ulrich Bez at the start of the project. The car had started life as a US-specification DB9 Volante and had been bought by American collector Peter Read, who had sent it straight to Zagato in Italy for its new bodywork. The car had serial number 14756.

The body was designed by a team working to Zagato's chief designer, Norihiko Harada, and the basic shape was the same as that of the special DBS coupé. It was intended to recall the iconic Aston Martins of the 1970s and 1980s, and among its more striking features were the front and rear designs. A blunt nose provided a suitably aggressive appearance and was matched by a squared-off tail, while the special tail-light units mimicked the design of the headlights. The interior, meanwhile, remained largely standard with the addition of stainless-steel trim and a green stripe on each seat that echoed the exterior colour.

After the centennial event in London, the car returned to the USA, where it was displayed on the concept lawn at the Pebble Beach Concours d'Élégance. Two years later, with just 3,700km (2,300 miles) under its wheels, it was auctioned off by RM Sotheby's at Monterey, attracting a winning bid of $693,000 (including the buyer's fee).

The DB9 Zagato Spyder Centennial was one of two special cars built for Aston Martin's 100th anniversary in 2013.

The Zagato Spyder's front end was unmistakably Aston Martin, but with a most attractive Zagato twist.

This rear three-quarter view emphasises the differences between the Zagato car and the standard DB9 Volante.

continued

continued

The soft top was sleek and tight-fitting, and blended perfectly with the lines of the car.

Side repeater lights were located in the wing strakes, above the signature Z of Zagato.

The Zagato interior treatment was not radically different from the standard Aston style, but it worked very well.

As its name suggested, the GT came with additional power: its engine had been tuned a little further to deliver 540bhp (547PS), although the torque peak of 457lb ft (620Nm) remained unchanged. These were figures very close to those for the engine of the DBRS race car, but of course this was not a race-car engine, but a higher-revving version of the standard V12. It drove through the standard six-speed paddle-shift Touchtronic gearbox, and the DB9 GT's top speed remained unchanged at 183mph (295km/h). There were improvements in acceleration, though: the 0–60mph (97km/h) time dropped to 4.4sec, the 0–100mph (161km/h) time was claimed as 10.2sec, and the standing quarter-mile time was reported to be 12.8sec.

The GT was unmistakable from behind thanks to a small GT badge next to the DB9 emblem on the boot lid, but there were other distinctive touches that appealed to aficionados. The front splitter and the rear diffuser were both painted black with all colours, or could be ordered optionally in carbon-fibre, and there was yet another new design of alloy wheels, with ten very slim spokes that exposed the brake callipers behind them. There was a choice of colours for these callipers, too.

THE DB9 HYBRID

As the electric-car movement gathered momentum, so Aston Martin supplier Bosch decided it needed an eye-catching car to demonstrate its latest hybrid technology. The German company approached Aston Martin and a co-operative venture was agreed. Work on the project began in April 2012, Aston Martin supplied a car to Germany in November, and the project was completed in May 2013. The car was announced to the media a month later.

Aston Martin made quite clear that the hybrid system was not destined for production, but that it demonstrated one possible future direction for hybrid sports cars, and one that fitted in with the Aston Martin brand values. Bosch, meanwhile, intended to use the car as a showcase for its technology, which depended on a modular design that could be adapted to the needs of different car makers and car types.

The white demonstration car retained its 6.0-litre V12 engine but also had two electric motors that powered the front wheels. These took power from a 180kW lithium-ion battery mounted ahead of the rear axle. The hybrid components added 300kg (661lb) to the overall weight of the car. The electric-only range was unfortunately as disappointing as in most electric cars of the time, and gave a range of little more than 25.7km (16 miles).

Nevertheless, Bosch's primary aim was to demonstrate the beneficial effects on performance, and they were keen to stress that the combined 740bhp of the petrol engine and electric motors allowed the car to accelerate from 0–100km/h (62mph) in just 3.7sec. In addition, the electric motors allowed torque vectoring for sharper handling, and the car was equipped with a four-mode Bosch ESP system that offered Safe, Sport, Drift and Custom options. In effect, it allowed the driver to fine-tune the steering, throttle, and oversteer or understeer characteristics, while taking account of tyre temperatures, tyre conditions and the number of passengers in the car.

For good measure, Bosch also equipped the car with a bespoke instrument cluster and a new infotainment system, both of which showcased other areas of their automotive business.

This publicity picture was used to promote the 2015 DB9 Carbon Black edition.

This door trim typifies the all-black approach to the interior of the Carbon Edition.

There had to be a special sill plate for the Carbon Edition, of course, and this was it.

Announced towards the end of the 2015 model-year, the DB9 GT brought extra performance and a striking appearance.

From the rear, the DB9 GT had an extremely satisfying all-of-a-piece look.

The alloy wheels with ten ultra-slim spokes were a distinctive feature of the DB9 GT.

The GT's tail badge was a discreet one mounted alongside the mainstream DB9 badge…

… and once again, there was a special sill plate for the DB9 GT model.

Then on the inside, the infotainment system had received a much-needed overhaul. The DB9 GT had a system that was an evolution of the AM II type fitted to the latest (second-generation) Vanquish models. This had a more user-friendly menu system, a useful text message readout function, Bluetooth audio streaming and a DAB radio. And because this was an Aston Martin, the system could also show power and torque readings in real time as well as check tyre pressures on the move.

In the UK, the DB9 GT was priced at the same £140,000 for either the coupé or the Volante convertible version.

CLOSE TO THE END: THE GT BOND EDITION

The link with the James Bond 007 film franchise that stretched right back to the mid-1960s was still strong by the time the DB9 was nearing the end of production, and the launch of the latest *Spectre* title in the series in October 2015 provided a perfect opportunity for another special edition. The film itself, incidentally, featured a specially commissioned Aston Martin called the DB10, which was never intended for production, and a 'reconstructed' Bond DB5 at the very end.

The Aston Martin DB9 GT Bond Edition really was a limited edition, and Aston Martin promised just 150 examples globally. Each one would be individually numbered, on the special sill plates that carried not only the James Bond 007 logo but also a reminder that this was a car that had been hand-built in Britain. The base car was the latest DB9 GT, and all the cars were coupés. All of them were also painted in Spectre Silver, which remained unique to the model. They came with 20in ten-spoke alloy wheels with a gloss black finish and diamond-turned spokes. The front splitter and rear diffuser were the carbon-fibre options from the DB9 GT, and the exhaust tailpipes had a dark Zircotec finish. Then

The GT Bond Edition was based on the DB9 GT. This one was pictured in Osaka, Japan.

As usual, there were special sill plates for the Bond Edition, in this case incorporating the 007 brand logo.

Completing the set of special features with the Bond Edition was a specially produced Omega wrist watch.

No detail was left unexploited... the 007 logo was embroidered into the interior trim.

there were sterling silver hallmarked badges on the wings, and some discreet 007 Bond Edition badges as well.

Obsidian Black leather was used for the passenger cabin, and the seat upholstery had straight fluting that was deliberately reminiscent of classic Aston Martins. Accents of Argento Grey welt and Galena Silver stitching avoided a sombre feel, creating instead a restrained and elegant ambience. The front head restraints were embroidered with the winged Aston Martin logo, and there was a 007 motif on the back of the centre console to remind rear-seat passengers that this was a rather special car. Even the start-up display on the dashboard's touch screen featured a reminder of the James Bond connection. A full-length carbon-fibre facia was matched by a special steering wheel, derived from the one in the One-77 supercar (and the DB10 film car), trimmed in Obsidian leather with Pure Black Alcantara inserts.

There was even a Bond Edition indoor car cover included in the £165,000 price of these cars, and as a finishing touch, each one came with a special handover case in blue box-grained leather with a Jacquard lining. The box contained a 16GB Bang & Olufson USB drive and an exclusive James Bond Limited Edition wristwatch, an Omega Seamaster Aqua Terra 150m timepiece.

And yet that was not quite all, because Aston Martin had one more special edition to deliver before they closed down the DB9 assembly lines for good. . . .

THE VERY LAST CARS

Production of the DB9 was scheduled to end in summer 2016, after nearly thirteen years and more than 16,500 cars – a figure that made it the most numerous of all the DB Aston Martins. The replacement model would be the DB11, the DB10 number having been reserved solely for the special film cars made for the James Bond film *Spectre* in 2015. However, Aston Martin chose to mark the end of DB9 production with one more special edition. Appropriately, there would be just nine of them.

That, at least, was the theory. In practice there were eighteen 'Last of 9' cars because the final production run was made up of nine coupés and nine Volantes. Seven of the convertibles had left-hand drive, which meant that only two were available for sale in the UK. All eighteen cars were painted in Cumberland Grey (a colour last used on an edition of the V8 coupé in the 1980s), accompanied by an interior with Bitter Chocolate semi-aniline leather that had a gold-coloured welt and thread. All the cars were also described as having special touches by Aston Martin's Q Department, which was so named after 'Q' in the James Bond films, who was responsible for creating all the hero's gadgets. Each 'Last of 9' wing badge was surmounted by a special 'Q' badge as rather amusing proof.

That, finally, was it. The official last day of production was on 26 July 2016, and the DB9 passed into history. But the car was certainly not done yet, and more than one aftermarket specialist recognised that owners might like to refresh their cars with some new features. The DB9 certainly did have an afterlife in the aftermarket, and some rather interesting confections were produced, though in fairly small numbers.

This press picture was issued to show the final nine DB9 models at the end of the assembly line. In fact, these were the last nine Coupés; there were nine Volante models as well.

The final DB9s had special wheels with a chromed finish and ten twinned spokes.

Special badging on each front wing distinguished the last production DB9 models.

The members of the Aston Martin workforce signed the cosmetic top cover of this V12 engine to commemorate the end of DB9 production.

The interior finish of the final cars incorporated Bitter Chocolate semi-aniline leather with gold stitching and welting.

There were special details on the centre stack, too: note the 'Last of 9' inscription on the control in the centre.

THE PROJECT KAHN DB9S

Project Kahn is a brand name of Kahn Design, a design company with premises in Bradford, Leeds and London. In the automotive world, the company has focused on visual customisation of high-end vehicles such as Porsche, Mercedes-Benz and Range Rover, and from 2008 it also offered enhancements for the Aston Martin DB9.

These early Kahn enhancements were marketed as DB9S items, and central to them was a six-piece bodykit that consisted of a two-piece front bumper spoiler, a two-piece rear apron, and a pair of side skirts. The combined effect of these add-on items was to give the car a more aggressive appearance from the front with a lower stance on the road. In 2021, this bodykit was still available at a price in the UK of £3,594 plus VAT.

Project Kahn offered several more possibilities for those who wanted their DB9s to look a little different. Options designed to go with the DB9S bodykit were a boot-lip spoiler and Kahn's own RS-V 20in wheels, with 9in rims at the front and 11in rims at the rear. These were designed to accommodate the original Aston Martin branded centre caps, and an additional option was a set of Kahn-branded valve caps. Pentagon privacy glass was available, and the facia could be given a high-gloss Piano Black finish with a matching steering wheel; alternative steering wheels came with a two-tone leather finish or a carbon-fibre finish. Kahn also offered their own Sport road springs and a Sports exhaust as part of the DB9S range.

While the cars remained in full production, that was enough to satisfy Kahn's customer base, but when DB9 production was coming to an end, proprietor Afzal Kahn saw an opportunity to create something very special indeed. The result very much polarised opinions, but enhanced the project Kahn reputation for producing cars that were deliberately intended as head-turners.

The first sketches and renderings of the Vengeance were made public in 2015. Kahn ordered five DB9 chassis from

The Kahn brand was dedicated to individuality and to going beyond the standard offerings of the specialist car manufacturers. This sketch showed their interpretation of the DB9, called the Vengeance.

Recognisably DB9, but quite different in so many respects, this sketch shows the rear view of the Kahn Vengeance.

This overhead profile of the Vengeance was used to promote the Kahn version of the DB9.

Aston Martin, who gave their blessing to the project, and promised a limited production run of unspecified length. As Afzal Kahn explained it at the time:

> *Aston Martin has always been an inspiration, in particular the early Vanquish and the V600 Vantage wide bodies, and I'm grateful for their agreement, and for wishing us success on this project. The Vengeance pays homage to those classic designs while using modern engineering to create something unique and original that reflects my own style. The Vengeance also underlines Kahn Design's expertise in design and coachbuilding.*

Arrangements to build the car were made with the same Midlands specialist company that had built the hugely expensive Aston Martin One-77 models between 2009 and 2012.

Actual release of the Vengeance was carefully timed for the Geneva Motor Show in March 2016, the very show where Aston Martin announced the DB11 as the forthcoming replacement for the DB9. It was a shrewd move: Kahn calculated that there would soon be owners of a DB9 who would be looking for ways of updating their cars. He had also made sure that there would be no objections from Aston Martin, and at the show the company's purchasing director Gary Archer was quoted as saying, 'There is a rich history of specialist coach-built Aston Martins. We wish Kahn every success with the Vengeance.'

The redesigned body of the Vengeance retained the overall proportions of the host DB9 but was designed to 'evoke the silhouette of a sabre tooth on the prowl', in the words of its creator. The most immediately obvious characteristics were the new grille and wheels, but a longer look would reveal more and more differences from the DB9 host car. The reworked chrome grille featured seven large vertical slats (the teeth of the sabre-tooth tiger) and was milled from a solid aluminium block. The alloy wheels had a design that suggested a roulette wheel, and had sixteen spokes with a 20in diameter at the front and eighteen spokes with a 21in diameter at the back, with 225mm and 335mm rim widths respectively and wide tyres to suit.

Every single exterior panel except for the roof of the original DB9 was replaced by a new hand-beaten panel in aluminium alloy. The roof, with a double-bubble design that deliberately recalled Zagato's trademark style, was bonded to the original roof panel in order not to compromise the integrity of the structure. The bonnet had a huge power bulge, and the new front bumper blended into flared and blistered wings that carried special badges. The doors were altered to give a wide-body look, and the rear wings were again massively swollen to cover the huge tyres, sweeping back to a tailgate and rear lights that took their cues from the Zagato DB7. Each car, promised Kahn, would have a plaque in the boot signed by every member of the team who built it.

It was no great surprise when the 2017 Geneva Show continued the momentum with a Volante convertible version of the Vengeance. However, it would be some time before any examples of the Vengeance were released to the media, and it was not until 2018 that both *Top Gear* magazine and *AutoExpress* were able to try examples of the Vengeance coupé in somewhat restricted circumstances. By then, four examples of the Vengeance had been built: the prototype coupé had been followed by one coupé for a customer and two Volante convertible versions. It also became clear that the prototype was not actually built from a DB9 but from one of the 2012-model Virage cars that followed it, and was in most respects an updated DB9. Prices were quoted, too, but were no doubt variable to match the individual specification of each car. *Top Gear* quoted £360,000 in January

Mansory started offering its own take on the DB9 theme as early as 2009, with the model it called the Cyrus.

2018, and *Auto Express* gave a figure of £400,000 in August the same year.

From the start, it had been Kahn's intention to focus on the coachwork alterations and not to attempt any mechanical enhancements – except for one. That was a baffle-free and outrageously loud exhaust system.

Ollie Kew's comments in *Top Gear* very accurately captured the point of the Vengeance. He said:

> *The only reason it's got an exhaust that'll be outlawed in Switzerland for potentially triggering avalanches is to make everyone within five miles wheel around to see what's creating the din. Which, if you've spent several hundred thousand pounds on new body panels for an old Aston Martin, is exactly the point. The sound, like the bodywork (coated in more glitter flake than a nursery arts'n'crafts project), and that dicey grille, are here for one simple purpose, to say:*
>
> *Oi, you there. Look. At. Me……This isn't a sports car. It's a billboard, a beacon, a giant neon arrow with fireworks, circus acrobats and pyrotechnics pointed directly at your forehead.*

It was more than successful at its appointed task, too. Kew added: 'It has now pipped any supercar I've ever been lucky enough to drive as the single most successful head turner.'

Auto Express agreed on the point of its head-turning qualities, but was rather more positive about the loud exhaust:

> *At full chat in third gear the Vengeance sounds like no other road car on this earth. It is cataclysmically loud, and the quality of the sound it makes is quite beautiful: a proper soul-stirring, heart-wrenching blend of pure volume – but also a clean, trumpet-like blare in the mid-range that gives way to a fully orchestral scream over the final 1,500rpm. The noise this car makes is enough to make the hairs on your neck go stiff with child-like excitement.*

There were, of course, some drawbacks. Kahn had done very little to the interior of the passenger cabin, and *Top Gear* pointed out that the ride was 'choppy' on those huge tyres, that the steering was now 'mired in inertia and kickback', and that the gearbox 'feels way past its sell-by date'. But, of course, such things were not the point of the Vengeance at all.

THE MANSORY DB9S

Meanwhile, DB9 owners on the European continent who wanted their cars to stand out among others had been turning to Mansory since 2009. This company operated out of Brand, near Bayreuth in Germany, and had initially been founded in 1989 to focus on the individualisation of top-end British cars. In 2007 it had taken over the Porsche tuning division of Rinspeed in Switzerland, and it had also developed enhancements for various BMW models.

The Mansory Cyrus programme worked on either the DB9 or the DBS. Options included an aerodynamics kit made of extremely strong carbon-fibre that added wing extensions front and rear along with side skirts and trim items. There was a redesigned front apron with enlarged air intakes, and a carbon-fibre bonnet panel containing a pair of slotted power bulges. Meanwhile, a redesigned rear skirt with integral diffuser contained the four stainless-steel tail pipes of a tuned sports exhaust system.

TECHNICAL SPECIFICATIONS: ASTON MARTIN DB9, 2013–2016

Engine (standard)
All-alloy V12 with 4 valves per cylinder.
5935cc (89mm bore x 79.5 stroke).
Four chain-driven overhead camshafts.
Compression ratio 10.8:1.
Visteon engine management:
510bhp at 6,000rpm
457lb ft at 5,000rpm

Engine (DB9 GT)
All-alloy V12 with 4 valves per cylinder.
5935cc (89mm bore x 79.5 stroke).
Four chain-driven overhead camshafts.
Compression ratio 10.8:1.
Visteon engine management:
540bhp at 6,750rpm
457lb ft at 5,500rpm

Gearbox
ZF 6HP26 six-speed automatic with Touchtronic 2 electronic shift-by-wire control system
or
Six-speed Graziano Trasmissioni manual.

Axle ratio
3.15:1

Suspension
Front suspension with double wishbones, incorporating anti-dive geometry, coil springs, anti-roll bar and monotube three-stage adaptive telescopic dampers.

Rear suspension with double wishbones with anti-squat and anti-lift geometry, dual-rate coil springs, anti-roll bar and monotube three-stage adaptive telescopic dampers.

Steering
Rack-and-pinion steering with standard power assistance.

Brakes
Ventilated carbon ceramic discs on all four wheels, with 398mm diameter at the front and 360mm diameter at the rear; six-piston monobloc callipers at the front and four-piston monobloc callipers at the rear.

ABS standard, with Brake Assist and Electronic Brakeforce Distribution; Dynamic Stability Control and traction control.

Wheels and tyres
20in (508mm) wheels with 8.5in (216mm) rims at the front and 11in (279mm) rims at the rear.

Pirelli P-Zero 245/35ZR20 tyres (front) and 295/30ZR20 tyres (rear).

Dimensions

Overall length:	4,697mm (184.9in)
Overall width:	2,017mm (79.4in) over mirrors
Overall height:	1,318mm (51.9in)
Wheelbase:	2,740mm (107.9in)
Track, front:	1,568mm (61.7in)
Track, rear:	1,562mm (61.5in)

Kerb weight

1,760kg (3,880lb)	Coupé
1,785kg (3,935lb)	DB9 GT
1,815kg (4,001lb)	Volante

CHAPTER 10

PURCHASE AND OWNERSHIP

First of all, it should go without saying that the Aston Martin Vanquish and Aston Martin DB9 are very special cars designed to suit the tastes and means of a relatively small group of people. They are not, and never were, intended to be everyday cars for the average driver. Like all Aston Martins, they are ideally suited to the enthusiast owner who will cherish them, use them fairly sparingly on special occasions, and can afford the ownership experience. And there lies a crucial issue. Ownership of one of these cars is not only about affording the purchase price – which of course has dropped very considerably since the cars were new. It is also, and arguably more so, about being prepared to fund the considerable maintenance costs.

Again, it should be obvious, but the average all-makes garage is not the place to have one of these cars maintained. Most such establishments would in any case refuse to deal with it because of its unfamiliarity. So an important element in owning a Vanquish or a DB9 is access to a marque specialist who understands the cars, knows what needs attention, and recognises early-warning signs that something may be about to fail. That kind of expertise does not come cheaply, but in the longer run it is likely to prevent catastrophic failures caused by neglect or ignorance.

It is important to remember that even exotic cars such as Aston Martins go through a period where they are treated as very much less than special: no longer fashionable, and old enough not to command high prices because newer models are more appealing, they go through their own equivalent of the 'banger' phase that affects all cars sooner or later. During that phase, many cars are not looked after to the necessary high standards, and as a result they deteriorate in sometimes alarming fashion and will later require major expenditure to return them to good condition.

Before setting out with the intention of buying an Aston Martin Vanquish or an Aston Martin DB9, it is sensible to read as much as possible about them – not only the relevant chapters of this book, but also every magazine article and internet report you can find. Some will be disappointingly lightweight, but others may give you the insight you need to decide which of the multiple specification variations will best meet your expectations.

Above all, spend some time just to go and look at cars that are offered for sale in order to get a feel for what is available. This may take several months, but it helps you to build up a store of knowledge that will ultimately lead you to buy a car that is what you want, rather than simply representative of the model. Only by looking carefully over several different cars, perhaps in widely differing price ranges, will you really get a feel for what makes a good example and what makes a bad one. Nobody likes a tyre-kicker, and you will do yourself no favours if you behave like one, but sellers are often quite understanding of an honest approach from a potential buyer who admits that he does not yet know quite what he wants.

THE VANQUISH

As the first of the New Era Aston Martins, the Vanquish certainly has a special place in the history of the company. It was the first 21st-century Aston, and the first to have at its heart that advanced structure that consisted of extruded and bonded aluminium plus composites. It also made the long-overdue break with earlier Astons by depending on a paddle-shift gearbox instead of requiring the driver to get used to the notoriously heavy clutch that characterised the late twentieth-century V8 models. It was also the last production car to come from the old Newport Pagnell works, and the last Aston to be so heavily dependent on hand-building (the DB9 was less hand-built than hand-finished, which is an important distinction for some people).

For those who consider buying an Aston Martin as an investment rather than purely for the pleasure of driving

The Vanquish was the first of Aston Martin's New Era cars, and its timeless style set the shape of the marque for the first two decades of the 21st century.

Still modern in appearance, although some of the equipment is very much of its time, the cabin of the Vanquish is one of the car's major attractions.

Hand-building touches show how much pride the company took in building its cars. This plaque is on the V12 engine of a Vanquish.

Huge disc brakes on the Vanquish guaranteed first-class stopping power in a car that was both fast and heavy.

Little details add to the pride of ownership. The engine of the Vanquish S was distinguished by a specially cast inlet manifold.

The Vanquish showcased modern hand-building at its finest. This is the interior of the first production car.

it, there are some persuasive figures associated with the Vanquish. Just 2,589 examples were built, which makes the car rare in comparison with a DB7 (around 7,500 cars) or a DB9 (over 16,500 cars) – although note that these figures are approximations because Aston Martin treats exact sales and production figures as sensitive information. This rarity is very likely to lead to an eventual increase in sale prices, and the association with the James Bond 007 franchise – the Vanquish featured in *Die Another Day* in 2002, as Chapter 3 explains – is also likely to ensure that prices remain firm. The 007 association has certainly done wonders for the prices of the earlier DB5 models over the years.

A few things deserve consideration before you set out with the intention of buying a Vanquish. First, these are heavy cars that weigh well over two tons with fuel and driver on board, and despite the quality of the suspension, brake and steering design, that weight is quite apparent and can persuade some people that the cars are not as sporting as they appear. Be reassured by the comment from *Evo* magazine in September 2001, which reported that the Vanquish was 'so fluid, so controlled and precisely damped, you're barely aware of all that weight at work through the bends.' There have also been questions about the car's use for track-day events. The standard brakes are more than adequate for all but the most extreme driving on ordinary roads, but they are not ideal for track use, and the cooling system's ability to deal with sustained hard use on the track has also been challenged.

One much discussed feature of the Vanquish is its semi-automatic gearbox, featuring paddle-shift control of an otherwise manual gearbox. Some people claim that they actively dislike it; others put up with it grudgingly. So it is worth remembering that the gearshift was improved for the later Vanquish S, and also that Aston Martin Works has converted a number of Vanquish cars to full manual specification, using the six-speed Tremec gearbox from the V12-engined DB7

The James Bond 007 connection gives the Vanquish its own special cachet. Here is 007 himself (Pierce Brosnan) in a publicity shot with an early car.

Vantage GT. No doubt they could still be persuaded to do so by anyone with the wherewithal to foot the bill.

First Considerations

The three most important considerations in buying one of these cars are overall condition, service history and mileage, probably in that order. Specification may also be a factor – and where a choice between manual and automatic gearbox is available, it may be decisive – but in genuine head-over-heart consideration it should probably be treated as less important. Colour is a matter for individual taste, but it is undeniable that some colours work much better than others on these cars, and that there is a reason why dark green and dark blue cars are much less common than silver, grey and black ones.

Maintenance is vitally important, and the cars are not tolerant of skimped servicing. The Vanquish requires a full service every 12,000km (7,500 miles) or twelve months, whichever occurs sooner, and to give an oil change even more frequently is a wise precaution. A fat sheaf of service receipts may be reassuring with a car for sale, but you should always check to see what was actually done and who did it. Ideally the car will have been looked after by a proper Aston Martin specialist, and if the papers reveal that servicing has been irregular, or that there have been long periods when nothing was done, be especially cautious. It is worth knowing that Aston Martin Works will inspect a car, road test it, and provide a full report on request – but of course the car has to be transported to Newport Pagnell first, and the report itself is not going to be cheap.

Structure

The carbon-fibre crash structure at the front and rear of the Vanquish can be seen from underneath, so it is always worth taking a look to see if there are any signs of damage or crash repairs. The carbon fibre can of course be repaired, but it needs to be done properly, and that can be expensive.

It may come as a surprise that corrosion can be a problem on the Vanquish. The most serious problems occur with the steel front sub-frame, because water gets trapped between this and the undertray, with inevitable results. The extent of any rust can only be properly checked by removing the undertray. There is also a small steel bracket at the end of each sill that can rust, and from here the rust may spread through the mounting bolts to cause an electrolytic reaction in the aluminium body structure itself.

Less problematic but also worth looking for are early signs of electrolytic corrosion in the aluminium body panels. Bubbling at the edges of the panels is an obvious warning sign, and of course the only remedy is for the panel to be stripped back, treated, and resprayed. Some cars also suffer from bubbling on the front wing strakes, although this only occurs when the strakes are cast items, which was not the case on all cars.

Mechanical Elements

The Aston Martin V12 engine is a long-lived and tough power unit that only rarely suffers from serious problems. Perhaps the most serious one is flagged up by a noticeable increase in oil consumption, because a low oil level can lead to crankshaft bearing problems. What happens is that the valves in the breather system stick open and the engine begins to consume its own oil vapour; the tell-tale sign is a heavy oil deposit inside the air filter – although a light misting of oil here is quite normal. One more common problem is with the coil packs, which can suffer heat damage or may short out thanks to water ingress. Trouble here may be highlighted by a misfire under load. The packs can be replaced one bank at a time, but even this is not a cheap job.

The paddle-shift gearbox in the Vanquish has received its fair share of criticism, some of it rather unwarranted. When in good condition, the gearbox offers a clean start from rest without noise or vibration. Software updates over the years improved the shift quality, and most of the early cars with analogue gear position sensors (which can wear) will have been updated with the magnetic sensors that became standard at car number 600. However, listen for a whistling sound, a warning that there may be wear in the spigot shaft, which will require expensive repair.

The clutch can of course wear, but the speed of that wear is inevitably dependent on the way the car is driven. Long-term Vanquish owners tend to reduce clutch wear by selecting neutral when the car is stationary for more than a few seconds, and it is always best to avoid allowing the car to trickle along in heavy traffic because that does promote clutch wear. In fact, guidance on this was interwoven with tuition about using the car's high performance on the one-day Aston Martin Performance Driving Course that was offered to every owner of a new Vanquish when the cars were still in production.

As noted above, the brakes are more than adequate for most purposes, but they do deserve a close look when examining a car for sale. The cross-drillings in the discs can become blocked, which in bad cases may result in corrosion. Regular cleaning as part of a service will prevent this from recurring.

The Interior

Despite Dr Bez's last-minute attempts to improve the quality of the interior before the launch in 2001 (see Chapter 3), the car has been regularly criticised for the poor quality of some interior materials. Some of the instruments and switches are recognisably related to those in considerably less expensive models from the Ford stable of the time (the clock was often criticised for its cheap appearance), and some of the aluminium-look trim is actually plastic.

The original Alpine audio system is not as highly regarded as the later 1300-watt Linn system (fitted to 2003-model and later cars), and cars with full leather (rather than leather and alcantara) upholstery and the two beautifully upholstered but admittedly useless rear seats tend to be priced higher than others without these features. Very much worth having, and perhaps a contributor to a higher asking price, is the Sports Dynamic Pack that was introduced in 2003 and brought improved brakes and suspension; the later Vanquish S of course had these improvements as standard.

THE DB9

At the time of writing, the DB9 was the most cost-effective way of getting into ownership of a modern, 21st-century Aston Martin, with prices starting at about half the cost of a Vanquish. That makes the car extraordinarily good value for money, but this bargain status cannot be expected to last forever. True, the Vanquish will probably increase its value more quickly on the grounds of its rarity, but as more and more DB9s are run into the ground by impecunious or careless owners, so the survivors will be more highly valued. The special-edition models from the later years of production will probably always be rather more expensive than the mainstream models.

Nevertheless, a temptingly low purchase price should not blind you to the fact that you are buying an Aston Martin, and that the car will need to be maintained in the appropriate fashion just like any other model from this famous maker. Fuel consumption is typically around 18.9ltr/100km (15mpg), rising to nearer 14ltr/100km (20mpg) on long motorway runs. Proper maintenance, with services every 16,000km (10,000 miles) or once a year, is fairly expensive – but it is less expensive than the major overhauls and repairs that will eventually become necessary on a car that has been neglected. High mileage on a car with a good service record need not prove a deterrent to purchase, even though the mileage may be useful as a bargaining counter.

There is plenty of choice for the would-be DB9 owner. Not only was the car built in large quantities (for an Aston Martin), but there were models with both manual and automatic gearboxes, plus a choice between Coupé and Volante convertible body styles. That said, the manual gearbox cars were comparatively rare, and there were very few Volante models with the manual gearbox. It is worth knowing, too, that the Volante loses a sizable section of its boot to the hood well, making it rather less practical for those who would like to use one as a weekend getaway car for two. Generally speaking, the 2009 and later models offer improvements that are worth the little extra that may be asked over a comparable earlier car.

Collecting sales material and other literature associated with the cars can be an absorbing adjunct to ownership of a modern Aston Martin. This is a DB9 press pack that was issued at the Dubai Motor Show.

The Body

The DB9 is of course built on the VH platform, a composite structure that moved on a step from the structure used in the Vanquish. Mostly made of aluminium, the body does not generally suffer from rust but it can suffer from aluminium corrosion in exactly the same way as the Vanquish body. It is worth checking the edges of the body for signs of bubbling under the paint, and it is a good idea to check the edges of the doors and the boot lid as well; bubbling can even occur around the door handles.

Paint issues should ring a warning bell. Matching the paint on replacement panels to that on the rest of the body requires considerable skill, and any evidence of a patchwork finish should suggest that the car has been damaged and repaired, probably on the cheap. Some of the early cars did have minor paint issues when new, but it would be a rare one that still survives without having been rectified to a very high standard under warranty.

The panels are bonded to the main structure and can be repaired if necessary, but only by specialists with the necessary knowledge and expertise. The bumper and front wings are lightweight composite panels and will be very expensive to replace. Check for stone chips around the nose of the car, and do not be surprised to find some evidence that earlier chips have been touched in. These are low-slung cars and may have grounded out on speed bumps and the like, so a good look underneath for any damage or signs of repair is also worthwhile.

It is of course important to check the condition and operation of the convertible top on the Volante models. The mechanism is electrically operated and should work smoothly, taking a claimed 17sec to raise or lower fully. The metal panel covering the hood well at the rear should also be a perfect fit. The convertible top itself is a multi-layer affair and durable in ordinary use, but that has never prevented envious individuals from wanting to inflict damage on it with a knife. Repairs to this kind of damage can be very expensive if they are not to be immediately noticeable.

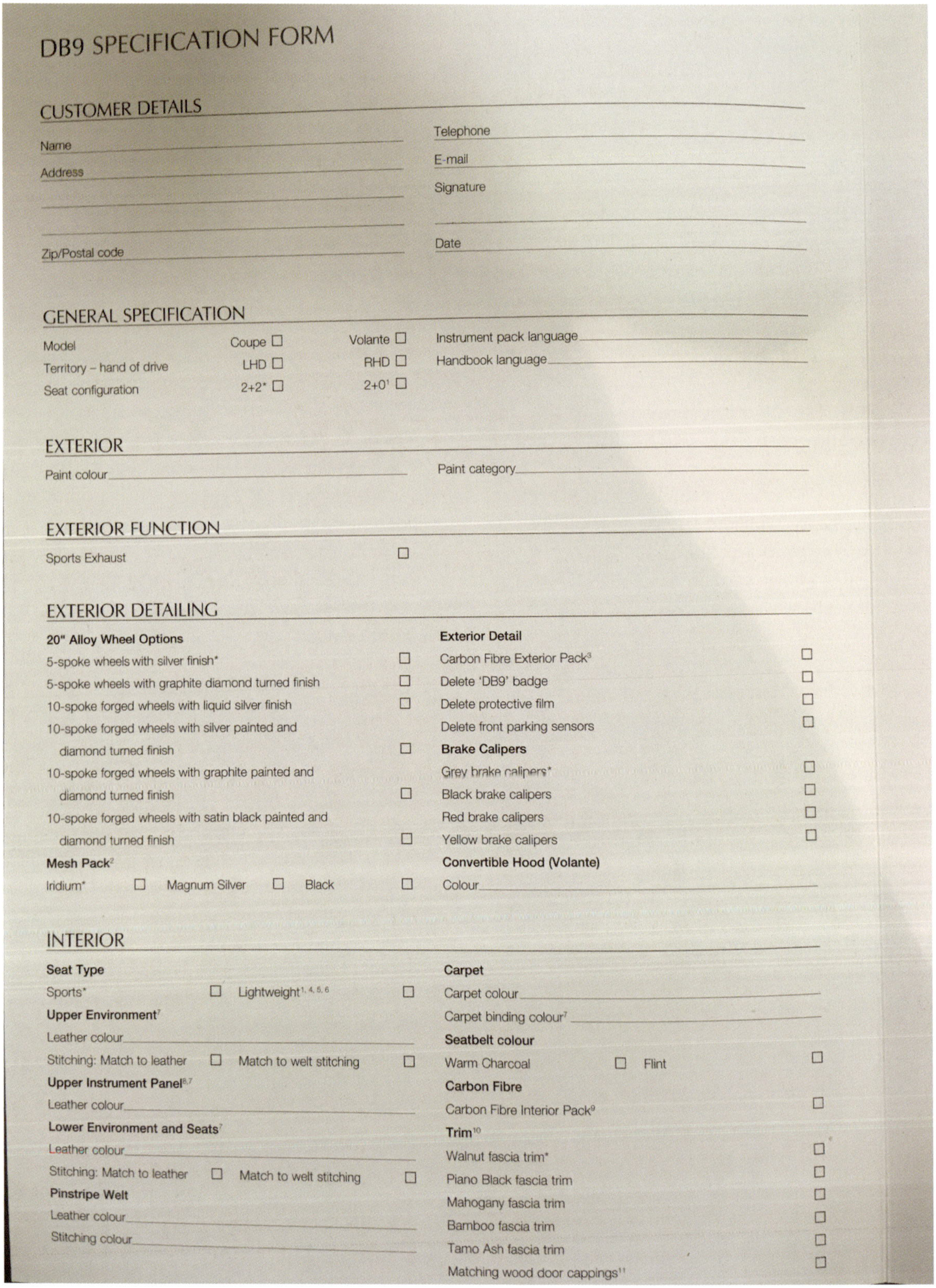

DB9 SPECIFICATION FORM

CUSTOMER DETAILS

Name ____ Telephone ____

Address ____ E-mail ____

Signature ____

Zip/Postal code ____ Date ____

GENERAL SPECIFICATION

Model Coupe ☐ Volante ☐ Instrument pack language ____

Territory – hand of drive LHD ☐ RHD ☐ Handbook language ____

Seat configuration 2+2* ☐ 2+0[1] ☐

EXTERIOR

Paint colour ____ Paint category ____

EXTERIOR FUNCTION

Sports Exhaust ☐

EXTERIOR DETAILING

20" Alloy Wheel Options

5-spoke wheels with silver finish* ☐

5-spoke wheels with graphite diamond turned finish ☐

10-spoke forged wheels with liquid silver finish ☐

10-spoke forged wheels with silver painted and diamond turned finish ☐

10-spoke forged wheels with graphite painted and diamond turned finish ☐

10-spoke forged wheels with satin black painted and diamond turned finish ☐

Mesh Pack[2]

Iridium* ☐ Magnum Silver ☐ Black ☐

Exterior Detail

Carbon Fibre Exterior Pack[3] ☐

Delete 'DB9' badge ☐

Delete protective film ☐

Delete front parking sensors ☐

Brake Calipers

Grey brake calipers* ☐

Black brake calipers ☐

Red brake calipers ☐

Yellow brake calipers ☐

Convertible Hood (Volante)

Colour ____

INTERIOR

Seat Type

Sports* ☐ Lightweight[1, 4, 5, 6] ☐

Upper Environment[7]

Leather colour ____

Stitching: Match to leather ☐ Match to welt stitching ☐

Upper Instrument Panel[8,7]

Leather colour ____

Lower Environment and Seats[7]

Leather colour ____

Stitching: Match to leather ☐ Match to welt stitching ☐

Pinstripe Welt

Leather colour ____

Stitching colour ____

Carpet

Carpet colour ____

Carpet binding colour[7] ____

Seatbelt colour

Warm Charcoal ☐ Flint ☐

Carbon Fibre

Carbon Fibre Interior Pack[9] ☐

Trim[10]

Walnut fascia trim* ☐

Piano Black fascia trim ☐

Mahogany fascia trim ☐

Bamboo fascia trim ☐

Tamo Ash fascia trim ☐

Matching wood door cappings[11] ☐

This original order form for a DB9 is an interesting reminder of how many decisions the buyer of one of these cars had to make when they were new.

DB9 SPECIFICATION FORM

INTERIOR (continued)

Steering Wheel
- Black leather steering wheel* ☐
- Colour-keyed leather steering wheel[7] ☐
- Black Alcantara steering wheel[1] ☐

Headrest
- Aston Martin 'Wings' headrest embroidery ☐
- 'DB9' headrest embroidery ☐
- Embroidery colour ____________

Rear Environment
- Aston Martin 'Wings' embroidery colour ____________

Headlining Outer
- Alcantara colour ____________

Headlining Inner
- Alcantara ☐
  - match to headlining outer
- Leather
  - match to headlining outer[12] ☐
  - match to lower environment and seat ☐
  - match to Pinstripe Welt ☐

Pedals
- Black pedals ☐

Sill plaque
- Personalised sill plaques ☐
- Hand built in England for – name to appear on plaque – up to 26 characters:

☐☐☐☐☐☐☐☐☐☐☐☐☐☐☐☐☐☐☐☐☐☐☐☐☐☐

COMFORT AND CONVENIENCE

- Rear parking assist camera[13] ☐
- Second Glass ECU ☐
- First aid kit[4] ☐
- Auto-dimming rear-view mirror*[4] ☐
- Auto-dimming rear-view mirror with garage door opener[4] ☐
- Trinket tray ☐

INTERIOR FUNCTION

- Alarm upgrade (tilt sensor and interior movement sensor) ☐
- Aston Martin Tracking by Cobra (UK Category 5 – standard in UK)[4,14] ☐

IN-CAR ENTERTAINMENT

- Aston Martin Premium Audio System* ☐
- Bang & Olufsen BeoSound Audio System (1000W) ☐
- Silver speaker grilles ☐ Black speaker grilles ☐

DEALER FIT ACCESSORIES

Wheel Accessories
- Valve caps with Aston Martin logo ☐
- Tyre cushions ☐

Car Protection
- Car cover – Silver with black piping ☐
- Car cover – BRG with silver piping ☐
- Car cover – Black with silver piping ☐
- Car cover – Dark red with silver piping ☐
- Car cover – Royal blue with silver piping ☐
- Winter wheels and tyres ☐
- Winter tyres ☐
- Carpet mats – two-piece set ☐
  - Colour ____________

Luggage
- Luggage set – Nubuck Black leather ☐
- Luggage set – Tan leather ☐
- Luggage set – Cream Truffle leather ☐
- Luggage set – Black Sports fabric ☐

Other Accessories
- Jaeger-LeCoultre DB9 Transponder watch[15] ☐
- Performance Driving Course ☐
- Aston Martin Picnic Hamper[15,16] ☐
- Battery Conditioner ☐

CONTINUES OVERLEAF...

* Standard
1 Not available for Volante
2 Includes lower front bumper and side strake meshes
3 Includes carbon fibre splitter, mirror arms, mirror caps, rear diffuser and black tailpipe trim
4 Not available in all markets
5 Must be ordered in conjunction with 2+0 seating configuration
6 Does not include side airbags and heated seats feature
7 Two colour rule applies – only two colours of leather choice available within the interior (excluding headlining and welt)
8 Only available in dark leather colours
9 Includes carbon fibre facia, door pulls and gear shift paddle
10 Only applicable if carbon fibre interior pack is not selected
11 Not available with B&O BeoSound audio system
12 Exact match not always available
13 Standard in US and Canada
14 Cobra is a registered trademark of Cobra Automotive Technologies SpA
15 Available to order through Parts Operations
16 Various colour options available

The glass start key on later cars is a wonderful piece of art, but can be fairly easily damaged.

The boot of a DB9 Coupé is quite big enough for most purposes, but the Volante loses space to its hood well.

The DB9 is quite sensitive to colours. Blacks, greys and silvers were always fashionable, but this early Coupé looks magnificent in red.

The clear and modern layout of the DB9's main instruments is a delight for drivers.

With the right combination of interior colours, the DB9's passenger cabin can look supremely luxurious, as it does on this Volante. Other combinations can provide a more Spartan and sportier ambience.

The pop-up satellite navigation system was often criticised for being rather clunky in operation. It was no thing of beauty, either.

This low-angle shot makes clear how attractive the DB9 Volante was. Not surprisingly, the cars are very much sought after today.

The Interior

Generally speaking, the interior wears very well, although there may be signs of hard use on the driver's seat bolster of a high-mileage car. The occasional creak or rattle is only to be expected, too.

It is worth checking that all the electrical equipment works as it should. The tyre-pressure monitoring system and the seat-adjustment controls have been known to play up, the electric windows have sometimes given trouble, and the Linn audio system was at one time known for not releasing CDs. The automatic gear selector should select Park when Park is selected, but was the subject of a recall on early cars when it failed to do so. The seats were heated as standard, and paperwork with a car may reveal that the control module has been replaced. In fact there were two factory recalls for this very problem on cars built between 2006 and 2014, where the module failed to shut off the heating elements once they had reached the designed working temperature.

From 2009, the cars came with the glass, stainless-steel and polycarbonate key that Aston Martin chose to call an 'Emotion Control Unit'. Many owners prefer to use the plastic second key that came with their car instead, because the glass in the elegant Emotion Control Unit is only too easily chipped. However, it is worth checking that the glass key is actually still with the car when considering a purchase.

The Engine

The V12 engine in the DB9 is essentially the same as the one in the Vanquish, and is similarly regarded as a durable, reliable power unit. The most common faults are electrical, and more specifically failures of sensors. Like its Vanquish counterpart, the DB9's engine can suffer from faulty coil packs, and trouble here is usually revealed by a hesitation or misfire under acceleration. It is important that the correct long-life sparkplugs are used, too: the difficulty of access to the two rear cylinders (which are below the bulkhead) means that these may not be replaced along with the others if servicing has been skimped and cheaper plugs have been used.

Oil leaks are not common, and are more likely to be found on a car that has been neglected or abused. These engines do use a little oil – about a quarter of a litre every 1,600km (1,000 miles) is normal – and it is worth checking that the oil level has been kept up to the mark.

The exhaust system was fitted with a valve that opens to give a distinct bellowing note when the engine is fired up, but closes to provide a quieter sound when the car is under way. Some owners adjust this (it is familiarly known as 'uncorking') to give a more dramatic sound all the time, but of course the value of that is purely a matter of taste. Also worth noting is that some specialists have offered lightweight flywheel conversions that are designed to make the engine more responsive.

The Gearbox

Most DB9s were fitted with the six-speed automatic gearbox, which offers paddle-shift control similar to that on the Vanquish, but of course actually operates very differently. The automatics are usually trouble free, although there was a factory recall for an intermittent fault which put the gearbox into neutral when the selector's chrome-plated surround shorted out against the printed circuit board underneath. The later Touchtronic 2 cars have a revised hydraulic control box that makes for quicker and smoother gearshifts.

The alternative six-speed manual gearbox may be the enthusiast's choice but was fairly rare: by 2010, it was being fitted to fewer than 5 per cent of all new DB9s. That rarity means that manual cars are likely to be more expensive to buy than automatics. The enthusiasts who bought the manual cars tended to use them enthusiastically, which of course led to excessive wear. Indications in a car's paperwork of very frequent clutch changes – at intervals of less than 24,000km (15,000 miles) or so – may be a pointer to this, and there may be further evidence in graunching noises from the gearbox – typically when second gear is engaged. Clutches should last for 32,200km (20,000 miles) or so, and clutch replacement is quite expensive.

The Suspension

The DB9 has double wishbone suspension front and rear, with coil springs, dampers and anti-roll bars. It does not normally give trouble, but clunks and rattles suggest a problem, while uneven tyre wear may be a pointer to poor alignment or to damaged control arms. The Sports Pack that was available from 2006 brought stiffer springs, with a lower ride height, recalibrated dampers and anti-roll bars, and lighter wheels. The result was handling that many people consider a big improvement over the earlier standard system. Further improvements were introduced in 2009, thanks to revised suspension bushes.

The suspension components are generally durable and do not require any special maintenance. However, suspension bushes do wear and may be the cause of unwelcome noises; they should probably be changed every five years or so. Stiffer bushes are available from aftermarket specialists, and these can improve the handling but sometimes at the expense of a harsher ride.

The Steering

The DB9's steering is a power-assisted rack-and-pinion system that is inevitably a compromise between ultimate sharpness and the more relaxed feel expected of a grand tourer. Early cars suffered from steering judder, which was sorted out by a factory modification. However, harsh kick-back remained an occasional problem, although it had largely been banished by the time the last cars were made.

Some other early problems were dealt with by factory recalls. Woolly steering resulted from incorrectly tightened bolts on the front sub-frame, and there were two recalls for replacement of the bottom suspension arm cam bolt, which could crack. Paperwork with a car should show if these recalls were carried out.

Wheels, Tyres and Brakes

Most DB9s were supplied with 19in wheels, although 20in sizes were available for later models. There was a variety of styles, and of course the choice from these is governed by individual taste. Tyres are also very much a matter for individual preference, although it is worth remembering that the DB9 is a powerful and heavy rear-wheel-drive car, and the more enthusiastically it is driven the faster its tyres – particularly those on the rear wheels – will wear. Around 16,000km (10,000 miles) between tyre changes is normal.

The same factors that cause accelerated tyre wear also cause accelerated brake wear, although in normal use brake wear is not an issue. Pads and discs are generally trouble-free, and 32,200km (20,000 miles) between pad changes is quite normal. The 2013 and later cars had ventilated carbon ceramic discs (and these were available earlier as an optional upgrade), but there was absolutely nothing wrong with the standard steel discs on the earlier cars. Nevertheless, some owners have complained of brake squeal.

COMPANIONSHIP

Ownership of an older Aston Martin is in many ways just like the ownership of any other treasured car. Owners tend to band together to share problems and experiences, and generally gain immeasurably from the experience. The club that welcomes the Vanquish and DB9 models alike is the Aston Martin Owners' Club (AMOC), which can be found on the web at www.amoc.org and also has a Facebook group (astonmartin.ownersclub) for social media users.

APPENDIX A

BUILDING THE DB9

THE GAYDON ASSEMBLY PLANT

When industrialist Sir David Brown bought Aston Martin in 1947, the company was operating from its traditional home at Feltham in Middlesex. However, the existing factory did not have the space for the expansion that Sir David wanted to achieve. He obtained the necessary space in 1954 by purchasing the Salmons-Tickford coachbuilding company in 1954, together with their premises at Newport Pagnell in Buckinghamshire and, of course, the company's traditional coachbuilding skills.

After a difficult period in the late 1970s and early 1980s, Aston Martin Lagonda was sold to Ford in October 1987. The new owners were understandably keen to make the most of their new acquisition, and made a start by drawing up the DB7, which they intended to build in much higher volumes than any traditional Aston Martin. However, the Newport Pagnell factory was not big enough to cope with such high production volumes.

The solution became clear in the early 1990s. Between 1992 and 1994, Tom Walkinshaw Racing (TWR) built the Jaguar XJ220 in collaboration with Ford-owned Jaguar at a new factory in Bloxham, near Banbury. When production ended, Ford secured this factory for DB7 assembly, which was carried out there between July 1994 and early 2004. At its peak, the Bloxham factory was building just over 1,000 cars a year.

Even that was not enough to match Ford's plans for the future of Aston Martin, and in the early 2000s the company decided to build a new factory and global headquarters for the sports-car brand. The site chosen was at Gaydon in Warwickshire, on a former RAF V-bomber base that had been acquired by British Leyland in 1978 and had since been developed as an engineering and vehicle test centre for the British Leyland group. Latterly it had passed to Ford, who had turned it into the engineering and test centre for Jaguar and Land Rover. Part of the site was also occupied by the Heritage Centre (now the British Motor Museum), the museum and administrative headquarters of the British Motor Industry Heritage Trust.

The choice of Gaydon was logical at a time when Ford was trying to bring all the British brands in its Premier Automotive Group together under the title of Aston Martin Jaguar Land Rover, which name was used for a while in the USA but never really caught on in Britain. Since those times, of course, Aston Martin has been sold into new ownership, but the company still retains the Gaydon site as its global headquarters. Meanwhile, the old Newport Pagnell site remains in use as the Aston Martin Works service, restoration and heritage centre, while the Bloxham factory has been sold on to new owners.

The Aston Martin Gaydon premises consisted of a two-storey office building and an adjoining production facility. It was opened in 2003 and was the first purpose-built factory that Aston Martin had ever owned, as well as by far the largest, being four times the size of the old Bloxham factory and offering the space to manufacture as many as 7,500 cars a year. There was further expansion in 2007, when a new design centre was opened next to the main building; this, too, was a 'first' for the company, as it had never before had a standalone design facility. This new area incorporated a 3D visualisation suite, a colour and trim studio, five axis milling facilities, a wood mill, a composite manufacturing area, and a showroom.

Today, Gaydon remains central to the Aston Martin business, but there has been further expansion. In 2015, the company purchased a site at St Athan in Wales – formerly the home of another RAF base – and built another new factory there. This opened in 2020 and was dedicated to production of the new DBX model.

Despite the major increase in production quantities at Gaydon, Aston Martin took great care not to lose the traditional essentially hand-built nature of its cars. Production of the DB9 was slow by the standards of modern mass production, and each car took around 200 man-hours to build, spending no fewer than 50 hours in the paint shop.

The production building was designed to provide a clean, clutter-free environment, and its ambience came from a combination of a gently barrel-vaulted roof with silver-clad walls, full-height glazing on one wall, and a polished concrete floor. In most modern car factories, cars are built on a moving assembly line, but the system at Gaydon was always different and considerably more labour-intensive. When series production of the DB9 coupé began there in January 2004, the system depended on a series of work stations where technicians assembled the cars with care. Once work had been completed at one station, the part-assembled car would be moved on to the next one, and so on.

The assembly process began in the BIW (body-in-white) area, where the body panels were bonded together to create the basic structure of the car. This area contained one of the only assembly robots in the whole plant. In honour of its function, which was to bond the panels together, and in honour of the Aston Martin marque's association with Britain's best-known fictional spy, James Bond 007, the machine was christened James Bonder by the assembly staff.

From the BIW area, car structures moved to the CMM Shop. The initials stand for 'co-ordinate measuring machine', and here each structure was carefully checked to ensure that the precise design tolerances had been maintained. The next stage was, inevitably, a visit to the paint shop, where the body would be painted to meet the customer's order.

Painted bodies then passed to the final assembly area with its series of work stations. Suspension, engines, transmissions, dashboards and interiors were all fitted here in a pre-defined sequence, and of course the upholstery was hand-stitched on the premises. At the end of the assembly process, each completed car was then put through a rigorously thorough inspection, and there was a small area set aside for vehicle rectification in cases where the required standards had not been met. (Aston Martin always took pride in pointing out that this was one of the smallest areas in the factory.)

THE COLOGNE ENGINE ASSEMBLY PLANT

The planned assembly process for the DB9 was not wholly in place when the cars were announced in late 2003, and in fact it would not be operational until a year later. In the beginning, the V12 engines were built by Cosworth in Northampton, just as they had been for the Bloxham-assembled DB7. However, on 20 September 2004, a new and separately branded dedicated Aston Martin Engine Plant (AMEP) was opened within the Ford plant at Niehl, a district of Cologne in Germany. In future, this would produce the V12 engines and would deliver them to the assembly lines at Gaydon.

The AMEP covered an area of 12,500sq m (135,000sq ft) and had the capacity to build up to 5,000 engines a year. With 110 employees, it consisted of three main areas: one to machine the cylinder heads, one to machine the blocks, and one to assemble and hot-test the complete engine. Just as was the case at Gaydon, traditional hand-building methods were retained in an otherwise ultra-modern environment. Each engine was assembled by a single technician from a pool of 30, and each one took an average of just under twenty hours to build.

PAINT COLOURS

The table does not include colours available for models other than the Vanquish and DB9, or special colours supplied to individual customer order. Note that some colours had more than one reference number.

2002–2009 SEASONS

	Ref no	2002	2003	2004	2005	2006	2007	2008	2009
Almond Green**	1339								
Amethyst Red*	1542								
Amethyst Violet*	5058D								
AML Racing Green	1140								
Antrim Blue	1114								
Arancio Borealis**	1635								
Argento Nürburgring	1137								
Aviemore Blue	1229								
Aysgath Blue	1230								
Balintyre Blue	1228								
Berwick Bronze**	1271								
Black	1106								
Blue Sapphire*	1346								
Bridgewater Bronze	1233								
Bright White	1630								
British Racing Green	1107								
British Racing Green*	1295								
Cairngorm Grey	1235								
California Sage*	1338								
Carbon Black*	1356								
Casino Royal*	1378								
Celeste Blue**	1335								
Chiltern Green*	1100								
Cunningham Blue*	1626								
Derwent Green	1159								
Elusive Blue	1334								
Emerald Green**	1625								
Ferrari Rosso Corsa	N/K								
Fire Red**	1377								

continued

continued

	Ref no	2002	2003	2004	2005	2006	2007	2008	2009
Ghillies Green**	1332								
Glacial Blue*	1532								
Glacial Blue 2*	5063D								
Glengarry Gold	1234								
Grigio Ingrid*	1125								
Hardly Green*	1649								
Ice Blue*	5059D								
Islay Blue	1149								
Jet Black	1328								
Jubilee Blue*	1636								
Liquid Gold*	1333								
Lightning Silver*	1535								
Magma Red**	5091D								
Mariana Blue	1540								
Marine Blue	1347								
Mendip Blue	1109								
Mercury Silver*	1300								
Merlot Red*	1342								
Meteorite Silver*	1344								
Midnight Blue**	1341								
Mombasa Orange*	9997								
Morning Frost White**	1362D								
Nemo Blue*	5074D								
Onyx Black*	1353								
Oyster Silver*	1340								
Pentland Green*	1113								
Quantum Silver	5073D								
Rathlin Red	1231								
Rothesay Red	1232								
Sarthe Silver*	5040D								
Skye Silver	1157								
Slate Blue*	1343								
Snow Shadow Grey*	0005								
Solway Grey	1150								
Storm Black*	1534								
Stratus White**	5057D								
Stronsay Silver	1104								
Sunburst Yellow**	1375								
Tempest Blue**	1374								
Titanium Silver*	1348								
Toro Red*	1302								
Tungsten Silver*	1262								

* metallic or micatallic paint
** pearlescent paint.

2010–2016 SEASONS

	Ref no	2010	2011	2012	2013	2014	2015	2016
Almond Green**	1339	■	■	■	■	■		
Amethyst Red*	1542	■	■	■	■	■		
Apple Tree Green	5126D		■	■	■	■	■	■
Casino Royal*	1378	■	■					
China Grey	5171D					■	■	■
Cobalt Blue**	5103D		■	■	■	■	■	■
Concours Blue*	5108D	■	■	■	■	■	■	■
Diavolo Red**						■	■	■
Emerald Green**	1625	■	■	■	■	■		
Glacial Blue 2*	5063D	■	■	■	■	■		
Grey Bull	5130H		■	■	■	■	■	■
Hammerhead Silver*	1125	■	■	■	■	■	■	■
Hardly Green*	1649	■	■	■	■	■	■	■
Jet Black	1328	■	■	■	■	■	■	■
Kopi Bronze*	5147D			■	■	■	■	■
Lightning Silver*	1535	■	■	■	■	■	■	■
Madagascar*	5127D		■	■	■	■	■	■
Magma Red**	5091D	■	■	■	■	■		
Magnetic Silver*	6005							■
Mariana Blue	1540	■	■	■	■	■	■	■
Marron Black**	5125D		■	■	■	■	■	■
Meteorite Silver*	1344	■	■	■	■	■	■	■
Midnight Blue**	1341	■	■	■	■	■	■	■
Morning Frost White**	1362D	■	■	■	■	■	■	■
Nemo Blue*	5074D	■	■	■	■	■	■	■
New Yellow**	5162D				■	■	■	■
Ocellus Teal*	5173D					■	■	■
Onyx Black*	1353	■	■	■	■	■	■	■
Quantum Silver	5073D	■	■	■	■	■	■	■
Scintilla Silver*	5156Z							■
Sea Storm*	5052D					■	■	■
Selene Bronze	5148D					■	■	■
Silver Blonde*	5079D	■	■	■	■	■	■	■
Silver Fox*	5131H		■	■	■	■	■	■
Silver Jubilee*	5136H		■	■				
Skyfall Silver 2*	5166D				■	■	■	■
Slate Blue*	1343	■	■	■	■	■		
Spectre Silver*	6008							■

continued

continued

	Ref no	2010	2011	2012	2013	2014	2015	2016
Storm Black*	1534							
Stratus White**	5057D							
Sunburst Yellow**	1375							
Tempest Blue**	1374							
Titanium Silver*	1348							
Tungsten Silver*	1262							
Ultra Marine Black**	5192D							
Viridian Green*	1666							
Volcano Red*	5151D							
White Horse	5137H							

* metallic or micatallic paint

** pearlescent paint.

Note: New Yellow was called Yellow Tang in some markets.

INDEX